Teaching Physical Education 11–18

Also available from Continuum:

Richard Bailey and Tony Macfadyen: *Teaching Physical Education 5–11*
John Beck and Mary Earl: *Key Issues in Secondary Education*
Sue Cowley: *Starting Teaching*
Nicholas Gair: *Outdoor Education*

TEACHING PHYSICAL EDUCATION 11–18

Perspectives and Challenges

Tony Macfadyen and Richard Bailey

continuum
LONDON • NEW YORK

CONTINUUM

The Tower Building, 11 York Road, London SE1 7NX

80 Maiden Lane, Suite 704, New York, NY 10010

www.continuumbooks.com

First published 2002

Reprinted 2005, 2006 (twice), 2007

British Library Cataloguing-in-Publication Data

A catalogue record for this book is available from the British Library.

ISBN 978-0-8264-5269-6 (hardback)

ISBN 978-0-8264-5270-2 (paperback)

Typeset by CentraServe Ltd, Saffron Walden, Essex

Printed and bound in Great Britain by

Biddles Ltd, King's Lynn, Norfolk

Dedication

To my parents for their love, support and kindness. To
Clive for all the laughs and the confidence he has given
me – I could never have started out with anyone better.
To Andy and Mike for their support and advice, cheers
fellas! To Rich, it's been fun, KMA! Lastly, to Sarah, for
simply being you.

TM

To my grandmother, Dora Sharrock, with love and
gratitude. Thanks Nan.

RB

Contents

Author Information

Tony Macfadyen is Head of Physical Education and Sports Leadership at the School of Education, University of Reading. He was previously Head of Physical Education at the Garden International School, Kuala Lumpur. His research interests focus upon talented pupils and leadership in sport.

Dr Richard Bailey is Reader in Education Studies at Leeds Metropolitan University. He works in the centres for Educational Research and Research Training, and Physical Education. He is author of a number of books on Education and Physical Education.

Tony Macfadyen and Richard Bailey have previously written the highly regarded *Teaching Physical Education 5–11* (Continuum).

Acknowledgements

We would like to express our warmest thanks to the following people for taking time to read and comment upon draft chapters: David Macfadyen (Saint Thomas More RC School, Eltham), Sarah Dean (Reading Girls School), Jon Tan (Leeds Metropolitan University), Andy Edwards (University of Reading), Wayne Richardson (St Peter's Primary School, Reading), Russell Jago (University of Reading), Mike Gray (Leeds Metropolitan University), Mike Osborne (University of Reading) and Jonathan Doherty (Leeds Metropolitan University). We would like to give particular thanks to Marilyn Pembroke for many hours of painstaking work in the preparation of this book. Any remaining errors are, of course, their responsibility!

Preface

Teaching Physical Education 11–18 aims to raise awareness of some of the critical issues and challenges facing the subject. In so doing, it aims to assist the teacher in the successful delivery of physical education. Drawing upon extensive research and wide experience, it offers the reader guidance in a range of areas that relate to good practice in physical education teaching.

As authors, we set ourselves the somewhat obvious but nevertheless important challenge of writing a book that would help teachers support pupils' learning. To this end, we asked ourselves two simple questions: what information would teachers need to enable them to reflect appropriately on physical education and what support would they want in order to teach more effectively? As such, the book contains chapters that consider key aspects of provision, such as planning, teaching methods, assessment and Special Educational Needs. There are also chapters on areas that are not often included in general texts, but which we felt were of enormous importance, like the place of the subject within the wider curriculum, talented pupils in physical education and subject leadership. It is hoped that the blend of chapters provides both a comprehensive and distinctive coverage of physical education.

As educationalists, we are fully aware of the requirements of the National Curriculum in England and Wales. However, we are concerned that there can be a tendency to confuse *is* with *ought*. Whilst many of us work within the framework of the National Curriculum, there is great scope for interpretation. Furthermore, we must not assume that its content and processes always represent the best ways forward. Therefore, we have set out to challenge received wisdom and provide alternatives. We hope that the separate chapters each make some contribution to debates within physical education. Together, we would wish that they make up a cohesive book that helps, guides and stimulates the physical education teacher.

Tony Macfadyen and Richard Bailey
University of Reading, Leeds Metropolitan University
September 2001

CHAPTER 1

Thinking about Physical Education in the Secondary School

'PE/Sport in schools is decreasing as a result of government initiative overload and National Curriculum pressures.'
Press Release, National Association of Head Teachers (NAHT),
4 March 1999

'A Sport England survey showed a huge decline in primary school children taking physical education lessons . . . Teenagers, too, usually stop playing sport as soon as they leave school. The figures are said to have alarmed ministers who are already concerned about the failure of the UK to produce new sporting heroes – particularly with Premiership football clubs relying ever more on foreign players.'
The Guardian, 15 July 2000, p. 7

'Physical education has been pushed into a defensive position. It is suffering from decreasing curriculum time allocation, budgetary controls with inadequate financial, material and personnel resources, has low subject status and esteem, and is being ever more marginalised and undervalued by authorities. At best, it seems to occupy a tenuous place in the school curriculum: in many countries, it is not accepted on a par with seemingly superior academic subjects concerned with developing a child's intellect.'
Hardman and Marshall, 2001, p. 32

Introduction

Why should physical education be included in the secondary school curriculum? What can it offer that is distinct and valuable? What should it encompass? Questions about the place and justification of physical education have inspired numerous writers and theorists (e.g., Arnold, 1979; Parry, 1998; Almond, 1997; Talbot, 2001). Alderson and Crutchley (1990) have suggested that, at a superficial level, everyone knows what physical education is, but beyond that the picture is less clear.

Despite the efforts of certain writers and professional associations (e.g., PEA, 1998), a lack of conceptual understanding of the term still exists. Some analysts have even questioned the wisdom of keeping the title 'physical education' at all (Singer, 1976; Wuest and Bucher, 1995), claiming that the label is not an apt term to denote the ideological or functional structure of the subject. The concept of physical education, it is claimed, is limiting and confusing, since it implies it is taught in isolation from thought and feeling and because education is a total and integrated process. Others have questioned the traditional ways in which physical education has been presented. Almond (2000, p. 4), for example, has called a physical education premised on skills, fitness and enjoyment 'impoverished and narrow'. Capel (2000a, p. 209), in contrast, claims, 'If physical education is only a list of activities, there are other people (such as coaches) and other places or contexts (such as extra curricular activities, community sport provision) which can provide opportunities for pupils to participate in those activities.'

Perhaps physical education teachers do not need to think about these issues. Some people may feel that it is inappropriate to spend too much time on these kinds of questions, and that too much philosophical reflection simply gets in the way of teachers' real work – to deliver the curriculum (cf. Parry, 1998). Other subjects do not seem to engage in lengthy defences of their place in the curriculum. One rarely reads, for example, of mathematicians or historians defending their subject with the same tone of self-defence and self-promotion as physical educators. The reality, however, is that physical education clearly does need to defend and promote itself at the present time. Evidence from the United Kingdom and around the world suggests that the subject is in an unprecedented period of marginalization (Hardman and Marshall, 2001; Speednet, 1999):

> At present (school physical education) suffers from a seriously declining infrastructure (provision and maintenance of facilities), a lack of advisory support and inservice training and inadequate initial teacher training . . . It is nothing short of a scandal that, as we rapidly approach the Millennium, PE and sports facilities in too many schools are not much better than those in a banana republic. (NAHT, 1999, p. 5)

In this light, justification is not merely philosophical play, but a matter of survival.

If physical education in schools were not under threat, there would still be a need for teachers to reflect on the justification of their subject. As professionals, they are obliged to engage in reasoned and public debates about the values and priorities of their profession. Even within a prescriptive statutory framework like the National Curriculum for England and Wales (DfEE/QCA, 1999), there remains scope for teachers, departments and schools to prioritize certain forms of experience over others, and to articulate a distinctive philosophy of physical education. Teachers' justifications of their work can act as summaries of the practical principles they most value; they are attempts to think through what the subject offers and should offer pupils.

Parry (1998, p. 41) has justified justification on two grounds:

- To defend and promote our subject; if we are not doing that, our justification is not good enough.
- To tell ourselves what we think we are (or should be) about. If we are not clear about our values and our direction, we need to think again about our justification.

He goes on to conclude: 'it seems clear to me that there is general agreement within the profession that we are not doing a good enough job in either of these areas' (Parry, 1998, p. 42).

In presenting the 'Case for Physical Education' at the World Summit on Physical Education, Talbot (2001, p. 39) lists six distinctive features of the subject which no other learning or school experience shares:

- It is the only educational experience where the focus is on the body, physical activity and physical development.
- It helps children to develop respect for the body – their own and others.
- It contributes towards the integrated development of mind and body.
- It develops understanding of the role of aerobic and anaerobic physical activity in health.
- It positively enhances self-confidence and self-esteem.
- It enhances social and cognitive development and academic achievement.

Few would disagree with these claims although the fifth point could surely be claimed by other curriculum subjects too. Yet physical education continues to be in a position of jeopardy. Moreover, many physical educators still struggle to define and justify their subject to colleagues, policy-makers and wider society.

This chapter considers some of the questions surrounding the place and value of physical education in the secondary school curriculum. It is framed within the context of a model of physical education originally suggested by Arnold (1979), and more recently developed by others (Bailey, 1999b; Williams, 1989):

- Education *about* movement.
- Education *through* movement.
- Education *in* movement.

It is certainly not intended as a definitive answer to the perennial questions outlined above. On the contrary, it merely serves to structure the discussion in order to raise some pertinent questions, and stimulate further thought and reflection. Ultimately each teacher needs to develop and articulate a personal philosophy of physical education, one that guides practice and the character of daily encounters with pupils.

Education Through Movement

Physical activities can provide a central point of interest and application for knowledge and understanding and may, therefore, be of great value as a focus for interdisciplinary studies. (Andrews, 1979, p. 18)

Traditional justifications for physical education have often been based on what Parry (1998) calls 'extrinsic' or 'instrumental' arguments. That is, they refer to the use of physical activities as means to achieving educational goals that are not inherently part of those activities themselves. Some of these traditional claims include the following:

1. Physical education for health and fitness.
2. Physical education for moral development.
3. Physical education for values education.
4. Physical education for citizenship education.
5. Physical education for aesthetic education.

The idea that broad educational aims and objectives can be realized through a well-conducted physical education curriculum is not new (Singer, 1976). What is new, however, is the range of learning to which the subject is expected to contribute: spiritual, moral, social and cultural development; literacy and numeracy; information and communication technologies; thinking skills . . . the list goes on.

Movement is particularly well placed to act as a medium for

learning across the curriculum, since it plays such a fundamental role in children's lives. Indeed, the psychologist Jerome Bruner (1983) suggests that action, play and movement constitute the 'culture of childhood'. It is through movement that children learn about themselves, their bodies and their environment, and movement-based activities can create a learning environment that is enabling and 'fun' (Bailey, 1999b). Daley (1988) claims that such activities are capable of generating empowering situations in which children relax and enjoy learning. By presenting learning tasks in physically active formats, teachers can encourage children who may have previously built up defences to lower their 'affective filters' (Gildenhuys and Orsmond, 1996, p. 105), their frustrations and anxieties, and start to enjoy learning.

Movement creates a meaningful context in which learning can take place (Bruner, 1983). Unlike a great deal of the secondary curriculum, where pupils read about events and concepts from a distance, in the context of movement, pupils learn by doing and being there (Bjorkvold, 1989). Almost every area of pupils' education can benefit from a movement-based approach, through introducing or reinforcing concepts, or giving practical examples.

Physical education's contribution to health has been utilized in a positive way to promote the value of the subject. Pupils' enjoyment of physical education can not only act as a catalyst to life-long physical activity (see education *in* movement), but health issues can also be taught very effectively *through* physical education. Indeed, aspects of health (and safety) occupy a prominent position in the National Curriculum for Physical Education (DfEE/QCA, 1999).

It is clearly important that the profession continues to highlight physical education's ability to prevent cardiovascular disease and other medical disorders in adult life (e.g., obesity, hypertension, osteoporosis; see Sallis and McKenzie, 1991; Morris, 1991). As a result of this, pressure on the National Health Service can be reduced and treatment costs cut. Furthermore, physical education can make an enormous contribution to the economy in terms of a healthier nation (e.g., in reduced days off work for back pain). As physical education's contribution to health is reasonably well documented (e.g., HEA, 1997), by way of illustration here, two other areas will be considered: language development and citizenship education (guidance on other areas of the curriculum can be found in Bailey, 2001a or DfEE/QCA, 1999).

Nowhere is the effectiveness of education *through* movement more apparent than in pupils' language development. In fact, movement does not just support the acquisition and development of language, it is an inherent aspect of it. A number of authorities agree that language is acquired and decoded through the integration and subsequent relationship between language and bodily movement (Bruner, 1983; Gildenhuys and Orsmond, 1996). Young children act out their conversations, and talk about their actions, as part of an inseparable partnership. As Bruner (1983, p. 4) puts it: 'language is orchestrated to the choreography of the human body'.

The scope of physical education as a medium for language development is vast. Hopper and colleagues (2000, p. 91) suggest that 'translating movements into spoken language in a variety of contexts offers a treasure chest of descriptive, directional and action words for children to explore and experience'. The activity areas – athletics, dance, games, gymnastics, outdoor and adventurous activities, swimming – each contain their own specific vocabulary and concepts. For example, gymnastics skills and agilities include travelling, stillness, balance, body shape, rotation, flight and inversion; and integral to these is a language of description, quality and expression (e.g., direction, flow, level, speed, range, relationships, timing and rhythm; cf. QCA, 1999).

Movement provides an environment in which learners are led to use language naturally and purposefully. Bailey (2001a) suggests some contributions that physical education activity areas can make to pupils' language and literacy development:

- *Athletics*: giving feedback on jumping actions.
- *Dance*: responding to poems, stories and rhymes.
- *Games*: adjectives and adverbs to describe movements.
- *Gymnastics*: describing the work of others.
- *Outdoor and Adventurous Activities*: reaching agreement in group problem-solving.
- *Swimming*: writing safety rules.

The relationship between physical education and what can broadly be termed citizenship education is less clear. There is a long tradition, originating in Victorian public schools, which argues that organized physical activities present ideal opportunities for young people to learn of success and failure, of overcoming obstacles, and of restraining selfish desires for the good of the group (Meakin, 1982). For many years some people have assumed that sports, in particular, are inherently moral enterprises, and offer players frequent opportunities to practise moral behaviour. Contemporary government reports have certainly endorsed this position. For example, in the report *Sport:*

raising the game (DNH, 1995, p. 2), the then prime minister, John Major, enthused:

> Competitive sport teaches valuable lessons, which last for life. Every game delivers both a winner and loser. Sportsmen must learn to be both. Sport only thrives if both parties play by rules, and accept the results with good grace. It is one of the best means of learning how to live alongside others and makes a contribution as part of a team.

In recent years such claims have taken on renewed importance as governments in many countries have demanded that all subjects, including physical education, demonstrate how they can contribute to pupils' values and citizenship education. Evans and colleagues (1996a, p. 8), however, have suggested that in the last ten years, policy-makers have put at risk many positive developments in physical education because of 'assumptions about the universal goodness of the properties of competitive team-games'.

In the most comprehensive review of the literature in this area, Shields and Bredemeier (1995) conclude that the research neither supports nor falsifies the claim that participation in physical activities develops appropriate values and behavioural traits. In fact, a more accurate summary would be that *some* studies suggest that participation can contribute to positive values development, and *others* suggest that it cannot (or worse, that it can actually be damaging).

Bailey (2000a) has argued that this apparent anomaly occurs because researchers have usually focused on the activities in which young people participate, rather than the way those activities were presented. It seems to be the case that the way an activity is presented to young people is at least as important as its specific content (Hellison and Templin, 1991; Biddle, 1999). Physical education lessons present numerous opportunities to discuss values and behaviour and have the significant advantage over classroom-based approaches as they occur in meaningful and valued situations (discussing fair play or teamwork has a unique relevance within the context of an actual game). These opportunities include:

- Discussing cheating in athletics; racism in sports; ability and disability; gender stereotyping in games.
- Problem-solving in Outdoor and Adventurous Activities.
- Helping to organize after-school sports clubs.
- Exploring different perspectives on bullying through dance.

- Examining representations of gender, race and ability in the sports media.

There are arguments, therefore, for physical education to be related to and interwoven with the full fabric of the wider curriculum. The notion of education *through* movement offers an opportunity for physical education to contribute to the overall character of a child's knowledge, skills and understanding, since it plays so fundamental a role in young people's general learning and development (Bailey, 1999a). Movement experiences are a fertile ground to create learning environments that are enabling and encourage pupils who have become disaffected with school to develop their skills and understanding incidentally as they engage in physical activity.

Can physical educators rely on these sorts of arguments to justify their subject? For all of the educational and personal benefits that might accrue via physical activity, and their current popularity among policy-makers, there are reasons to suppose that justifying physical education purely in terms of education *through* movement will be inadequate. This is because justifications of this sort refer to something that is outside physical activity or movement, and claim that activity can be used as an instrument to promote the values of that other thing (Parry, 1998). Therefore, it is not physical education or physical activity that is being justified, but instead language, citizenship or moral development. Physical education is the means, not the end of the enterprise; its justification is contingent on a more fundamental educational goal. If policy-makers can find cheaper or more effective ways of achieving the same outcome, there is no need to keep physical education in the curriculum at all. Likewise, if it cannot be shown that physical education contributes to these outcomes (as may be the case with moral development), then its justification becomes precarious.

It needs to be stressed that none of the previous discussion should be understood as a rejection of the contribution that physical education can make to the wider curriculum. On the contrary, it is fully acknowledged that movement can significantly enhance the quality of learning in all curricular areas. If physical education's position within the school day is strengthened as a result of instrumental, extrinsic arguments, all the better. However, the physical education profession should proceed with care; as Parry (1998, p. 46) has cautioned:

> . . . the tail should not wag the dog. We should be interested
> first and foremost in our own principled view of PE and should

seek to incorporate instrumental values to suit our purposes, not someone else's. To do otherwise would be to accept overt or latent political direction. Instrumental justifications, though sometimes useful if sensibly deployed, must be seen as at best ancillary benefits to a subject which stands or falls by the strength of its primary rationale, which will be intrinsic and educational.

The search for persuasive arguments for physical education should never lose sight of the subject's uniqueness; the contribution that it, alone, can make to a child's education and development. Therefore, what is needed is some form of 'intrinsic' justification, which focuses on the educational benefits of movement and physical activity, irrespective of their contribution to other educational goals.

Education *About* Movement

If the very best of our culture is to be made accessible to all young people, we need to ensure that we provide the means of engagement in such cultural activities so that young people can come to understand the scope of human endeavour and learn to recognise their significance. (Almond, 2000, p. 4)

Part of physical education's role is to introduce pupils to a range of physical activities, as well as the concepts, rules and procedures associated with them. Its value, in part, is in exposing pupils to new, culturally important, experiences that they might not otherwise have. Familiarizing pupils with the skills that make up different activities is an important objective 'because sport is a product of the social system and is related to culture, the student should have the opportunity to become conversant with it' (Singer, 1976, p. 54). In learning *about* movement, it is important that children are able to make informed decisions concerning activities that can enrich their lives.

Of course, there are many physical activities that pupils might experience, and each can make a distinctive contribution to their development and understanding. The National Curriculum for England and Wales (DfEE/QCA, 1999), for example, offers the following activity areas as the basis of statutory physical education provision:

- Games
- Gymnastics

- Dance
- Swimming
- Athletics
- Outdoor and adventurous activities.

It also outlines the knowledge, skills and understanding in which pupils are expected to make progress, through each activity area:

- Acquiring and developing skills.
- Selecting and applying skills, tactics and compositional ideas.
- Evaluating and improving.
- Knowledge and understanding of fitness and health.

In learning *about* movement, it is important that pupils come to know the range and character of the forms of physical activity. Actual physical performance of these activities is the central aspect of this knowledge. By taking part in different structured activities, pupils can come to know *how* to move in particular situations to achieve certain outcomes. At the same time, they also need to come to know *that* some ways of moving offer success or are more aesthetically pleasing than others. An adequate physical education must encompass both kinds of knowledge: knowing *how* (to perform certain skills and techniques) and knowing *that* (for example, orienteering requires the development of map-reading, compass work and physical geography).

Different children enjoy and succeed in different activities, so it is important that the scope of the physical education curriculum provides sufficient breadth and balance to engage all pupils. Some critics have questioned whether schools really do offer pupils a broad and balanced curriculum (Lockwood, 2000). Numerous surveys have reported that games teaching takes up a large proportion of curriculum time compared to each of the other areas. Fairclough and Stratton (1997), for example, found that games received the largest amount of curriculum time throughout Key Stages 3 and 4 (followed by athletics, dance and swimming). Within the games provision, traditional team sports, such as rugby, football and hockey, dominated the curriculum throughout Years 7 to 11. Similar results were found by Penney and Evans (1994) and OfSTED (1995), who reported that between 50 and 70 per cent of physical education time was taken up with games.

This dominance of games within the physical education curriculum has a long history (Lockwood, 2000). Indeed, the bias towards games was even written into statute in the original National Curriculum for Physical Education (DES/WO, 1992). Reflecting on this situation, Evans and colleagues (1996a, p. 7) wrote that the:

> . . . text of the NCPE (National Curriculum for Physical Education) now reinforces a very narrow and 'traditional' definition of physical education as comprising a set of separate and distinct areas of activity and openly accords the highest status to that area that long dominated the physical education curriculum in state schools, namely, competitive team games. Nowhere does the text prompt teachers to reflect on present provision, or consider how or why they teach.

The result of this emphasis on just one activity area means that the range of experiences offered to pupils during their formal schooling may be limited. Biasing physical education provision in favour of competitive games also means biasing provision *against* all of the other activity areas. A narrow conception of a curriculum centred on competitive team games threatens to alienate a large proportion of the school population, as well as deny them valuable learning experiences.

Nixon and Jewett (1974) have asserted that physical education should aim to make a maximal contribution to the optimal development of an individual's potential *in all phases* of life. Consequently, one of the key objectives of physical education should be to 'develop skills, knowledge and attitudes essential to satisfying, enjoyable physical recreation experiences engaged in voluntarily throughout one's lifetime' (Nixon and Jewett, 1974, p. 51). There is evidence that competitive games has limited appeal to many pupils, especially girls (Penney and Evans, 1997), and that secondary school physical education provision is disturbingly unsuccessful at instilling a long-term interest in physical activity (Kay, 1995; Macfadyen, 1999). To some extent this is because the physical education curriculum does not adequately reflect the sorts of activities in which young people are likely to participate in later life:

> There is a discontinuity between the types of activities which girls are most likely to have been introduced to through school sport, and the activities which they might expect to take part in as leisure in adulthood . . . For girls, many sport experiences at school are unlikely to be seen as relevant to later life; in the adult world, the activities traditionally offered to schoolgirls do

not enjoy either mass participation or elite status of boys'
football, cricket and rugby, and role models are few. P.E.
activities can be viewed as 'childish', and the transition to
female adulthood is more likely to involve leaving sport behind
than continuing it. (Kay, 1995, p. 61)

In a similar light, some writers have questioned whether physical
education, as currently conceived and presented, can offer any
meaningful or valuable opportunities to pupils with physical or
learning difficulties. Barton (1993), for example, has expressed
doubts that the curriculum is premised on an enabling view of
disability. He argues that important issues still need to be considered
if all pupils are really going to receive a worthwhile physical education on an equal basis with their able-bodied peers. He suggests
that the following points need to be considered:

- Physical education is the creation of and for able-bodied people.
- It gives priority to certain types of human movement.
- Individual success is viewed as a means of personal status and
  financial well-being; it is depicted as a way to the 'good life'.
- A whole consumer industry has been generated around such
  activities; sport has become a commodity to be sold in the
  market-place.
- The motivation to participate is encouraged through the artic-
  ulation of idealized notions of normality.
  (Barton, 1993, p. 49)

Narrow, traditional, games-orientated conceptions of physical education present barriers to participation beyond any that might result
from the pupil's condition. The physical education curriculum itself
can be accused of disabling pupils (Bailey and Robertson, 2000), and
this means that there is likely to be little connection between school
experience and adult physical activity.

If young people are to continue with physical activity after they
leave school, it will need to have deep personal significance for them.
It seems logical, therefore, that pupils should be allowed to explore
a wide range of activities in order to find those that suit their
particular abilities, characters and interests. The competition inherent in games is of a very different nature to the expressiveness and
self-direction of dance, and each has the potential to produce their
distinctive experiences and satisfactions that allow individuals to
explore different ways of moving or of being physically active. This
seems to suggest that the physical education curriculum in secondary

schools should aim to strike a balance between introducing pupils to new and varied movement experiences, and allowing them to build up a relationship with those activities that interest them most.

Education *in* Movement

Now anyone who has managed to get to the inside of what is passed on in schools . . . will regard it as somehow ridiculous to be asked what the point of the activity is. The mastery of the 'language' carries with it its own delights . . . But for a person on the outside it may seem difficult to see what point there is in the activity in question. Hence the incredulity of the unini-tiated when confronted with the rhapsodies of the mountain-climber, musician or golfer. Children are to a large extent in the position of such outsiders. The problem is to introduce them to a civilised outlook. (Peters, 1966, p. 255)

Education *in* movement is the most fundamental dimension of the physical education curriculum as it concerns introducing pupils to a 'physical' dimension, which is included in the curriculum for its intrinsic value and for the satisfaction that such movement experiences bring. Through engaging in physical activities and exploring the possibilities and the limitations of those activities, pupils can come to experience them from the 'inside' rather than as disinterested observers, as Peters' quotation indicates. Pupils go beyond simply engaging in activities to come to appreciate them and learn from engaging in them (Almond, 1997).

An important function of physical education must be to inspire pupils with a love of different forms of physical activities. They are activities and experiences that are valuable *in their own right*, and it is this unique focus of interest that helps make physical education distinctive and worth while. Owen (1968, p. 45) suggests that physical education might best serve a pupil 'by extending his knowledge and perception of what it means, in the fullest human sense, to have a physical existence'. Encouraging pupils to enjoy the intrinsic value of movement, and fostering a passion for physical activity that extends into participation for life, could be one of the biggest services that physical education could do for young people.

Moving forward

A number of factors would seem to follow from the previous discussion. First, to constitute physical *education* rather than just physical *training*, pupils need to engage in their activities in some cognitive, as well as performative, way. The National Curriculum (DfEE/QCA, 1999, p. 23) encourages pupils to 'select and apply skills, tactics and compositional ideas', to 'evaluate and improve', and to develop 'knowledge and understanding of fitness and health'. Each of these strands requires thought: pupils need to plan ahead, and reflect on their actions. These themes cannot be separated from the performance of skills and activities (Clay, 1997). However, there may be situations when it may be appropriate to focus on the more intellectual aspects of an activity. Some pupils may find it difficult to excel in the performance of a skill, but can reveal high levels of knowledge and understanding in choreographing a dance, or in observing and coaching others, so it is important that the teacher values the different aspects of physical education. Bailey (2001a, p. 7) reports a comment made by a head of physical education in a secondary school, after broadening the focus of teaching to empha-size and value leadership, planning and evaluating skills, alongside performance:

> All of a sudden, pupils who had thought that PE wasn't for them because they couldn't perform the skills well were getting praise and being valued by peers in lessons. They started realizing that they could make their own contribution to the lesson, and that it was valuable and appreciated.

Likewise, Ruddock and colleagues (1994) suggest that consideration of the concept of coherence may be better viewed from the perspective of individual meanings rather than common structures, so pupils come to see an overall meaning and have confidence in the relevance of their physical education.

Second, Prochaska and Marcus' 'Transtheoretical Model' of readiness for physical activity (1994) suggests that people are differently predisposed to exercise. Children have their own unique timing and pattern of growth and development which can affect their attitude to movement. Rowland (1991) has suggested that young people have a keenness to be active powered by a central drive mechanism that declines in adolescence. If children are differently affected by this drive, as one would expect, a 'one-size-fits-all' policy towards participation is clearly inadequate, especially as physical education is taught in such a public domain, and puberty and adolescence can make secondary education a sensitive time. Research by Cockburn (2001) found that girls admitted to not taking their physical education kit to lessons because they did not always want to do physical education or because their individual preference for physical activity did not match what was provided. In such cases the teacher needs to work with these pupils to foster an appreciation of the importance of movement and physical activity in a way that is meaningful to them.

Third, it must be of concern that physical education sometimes forces pupils to participate in activities they may not enjoy, in unpleasant climatic and environmental conditions. The credibility of physical education as the basis for life-long physical activity will clearly be tested by playing hockey in cold conditions on a rough surface that makes learning difficult and dangerous and leads many pupils only to feel uncomfortable and frustrated. Likewise, a cross-country run through wet, muddy conditions may seem to bear little resemblance to many pupils' future activity plans and thus does not appear very supportive to pupils. Indeed, these examples seem destined to lead to further negative feelings being associated with physical activity and consequently less chance of pupils being active for life. The approach needs to be sympathetic, positive, relevant and imaginative if physical education is to avoid becoming *physical miseducation*!

Fourth, it seems to be essential that older pupils are given opportunities to select from a choice of activities. As McConachie-Smith (1996, p. 89) indicates

> By Key Stage 4 the individual pupil is ready to appreciate the deeper meanings and successes of taking part seriously in activity; and this will only be truly experienced where each individual can become engaged in activities the demands of which can be well matched by the individual's expertise. Freedom to choose . . . is therefore of critical importance.

This is supported by Coakley and White (1992) who found that lack of choice in school physical education was associated with limited participation in community sport programmes.

Conclusion

This chapter has considered a number of issues concerning the place and value of physical education in pupils' schooling. It has been suggested that physical activities, both formal and informal, form significant elements within our culture, as well as within the very notion of being a human being. As such, physical education in some form would seem to be a valuable, necessary and integral part of the secondary school curriculum. However, the importance of physical education has not always been recognized. The philosophically minded might attribute this predicament to an exaggerated separation of the mind and body, in which physical matters are placed a poor second. This lies at the heart of Williams' (1989, p. 19) statement:

> The paradox with which we are faced is that while it is the physical nature of the subject which gives it its distinct identity and its unique place in the curriculum, it is this very physical nature which places it at the periphery of the curriculum.

The suggestion made in this chapter is that physical education has a unique and significant contribution to make to the overall education of every child because of its physical character. If the potential and range of the physical education experience is not fully realized in practice, then pupils cannot be said to be properly educated.

CHAPTER 2

Promoting Positive Learning

Introduction

The learning environment is the social context in which learning takes place, and it can have a considerable influence on pupil learning and behaviour during lessons (Wragg, 1984). A range of factors contribute to the development and maintenance of a learning environment, such as teachers' styles of communication, their expectations, their responses to events and the values that they promote through their teaching (Lambirth and Bailey, 2000).

It is essential that physical education lessons are characterized by a positive climate that supports learning and achievement for all pupils, as Rink (1993, p. 127) testifies: 'Physical Education classes should be characterised by an environment that is conducive to learning. Gymnasiums should be places where all students can have positive experiences. Teachers and students should enjoy being there.'

However, it is worth remembering that not all people look back on their physical education lessons as positive experiences. Indeed, the aggressive, insensitive and excessively strict physical education teacher has become a well-worn cliché in films and on television. Most physical educators, predictably, enjoyed their experiences at school, and it can be difficult for them to acknowledge others' difficulties. Research, however, suggests that negative memories of physical education lessons – boredom, lack of choice, being made to feel stupid and incompetent (Coakley and White, 1992; Macfadyen, 1999) – can lead to negative feelings being associated with physical activity in general. Such feelings can, in turn, result in a reluctance to participate in any physical activity after leaving school (Mason, 1995).

This chapter considers the significance of a positive learning environment in physical education lessons, and suggests strategies for developing and maintaining social contexts that promote learning, motivation, respect and personal achievement.

Positive Climates

The climate of a lesson is its general atmosphere or tone. A positive climate engages and motivates pupils, gains their co-operation and respect, and creates a working environment orientated towards learning and achievement. Negative climates, in contrast, stress coercion and punishment. In the positive form, the teacher is viewed as a facilitator of learning or a resource; in the latter, the teacher has an adversarial role. In almost all educational contexts, positive climates are more effective and sustainable. They also engender a more enjoyable and satisfying environment for both teachers and learners.

Successful physical education lessons that are taught in a positive, purposeful and task-orientated manner are likely to be motivating and enjoyable experiences for learners. Pupils' views of a good teacher are strikingly similar to those of teachers themselves. One study (reported in Cohen *et al.*, 1996) of the views of Scottish twelve-year-olds found that pupils regarded favourably teachers who keep order, are strict and punish pupils, actually teach and keep pupils busy with work, give explanations, are helpful and can be understood, are interesting, unusual and different, are fair, consistent and have no favourites, and are friendly, kind, talkative and jovial. Teachers' views would probably be in general agreement with these pupils' model of a good teacher (Wragg and Wood, 1984b). In his review of research on pupils' descriptions of 'good' teachers, Saunders (1979) came to conclusions that reflect theorists' views very closely indeed (Mawer, 1995; Rink, 1993):

Pupils think that good teachers:

- Are purposeful and in control of themselves.
- Know what they want to teach and check that the pupils are learning.
- Take positive action when they discover pupils are not making adequate progress.

- Are sensitive to the reactions of the pupils and respond by changing role smoothly and appropriately.
- Try to understand the point of view of the learner.
- Show respect for others.
- Are concerned for all pupils.

In other words, according to pupils' accounts, good teachers manage to combine purposefulness and sensitivity.

Underpinning this account of a good teacher is a particular conception of an appropriate relationship between teacher and pupils. The teacher needs to be 'confident, authoritative and clearly in control of the situation' (Capel *et al.*, 1997, p. 100), but also sensitive to pupils' needs and individual differences. This can be a difficult balance to strike: a teacher who acts in a strong and authoritative manner but fails to show value and respect for learners can come across as insensitive and cold; conversely, the teacher who succeeds in expressing respect for pupils' differences and needs, but is unable to remain in control of the lesson, may seem weak and ineffectual. Research shows that effective teachers relate to their pupils in ways that stress their positive regard for them, and they strive to take account of individual differences among the class, even when teaching large groups. These teachers also encourage active participation in lessons, use praise and create conditions that help to encourage pupils to perform well.

Simply being a teacher empowers an individual with certain institutional authority and legal powers. However, teachers rarely receive the same level of respect as they once did. As Tattum (1982) puts it:

> Respect for the teacher *qua* teacher can no longer be assumed as a social fact. No longer is the office held in awe and teachers who draw heavily upon unquestioned authority as an endowed right leave themselves open to mimicry and ridicule.

There are a number of strategies available for teachers which support the development of appropriate relationships with pupils, such as:

- Learn pupils' names.
- Listen to pupils' ideas, and involve them in decision-making, when appropriate.
- Be consistent.
- Develop a sense of belonging and group responsibility within a class.

Most fundamentally, a teacher's authority and respect rests on the establishment of a purposeful learning environment, effective teaching skills, together with the concern shown for pupils and their welfare.

Engagement in Learning

An important skill in maintaining a purposeful learning environment includes monitoring pupils' involvement in the planned activities, and correcting them when they depart from them. All pupils, from time to time, are likely to be distracted from a task and, of course, some are more liable to do this than others. Some may have become 'competent bystanders' (Siedentop, 1991): they may appear to be fully engaged in an activity, but in fact they are subtly avoiding participation. Others may enthusiastically be participating in a different task than has been planned. There is a danger of tolerating these sorts of behaviours as long as pupils seem to be physically active and well behaved, which is sometimes called the 'busy, happy and good syndrome' (Placek, 1983). This approach may be appealing, but it is inadequate since it places learning in a position of incidental importance behind a superficial image of physical activity. When this situation arises, physical education becomes little more than a supervized break-time.

It is a truism that the more time learners participate in a learning experience, the more opportunities they have to learn. Some writers use the phrase 'Academic Learning Time' (ALT) which is 'the amount of time a student spends on an academic task he/she can perform with high success. The more ALT a student accumulates, the more the student is learning' (Fisher et al., 1980, p. 8). This conception has been enthusiastically picked up by physical education theorists, who have translated it to Academic Learning Time in Physical Education (ALT-PE; Metzler, 1989), and have developed observational tools to record learning time (cf. Mawer, 1995). Generally speaking, research using ALT-PE observations has provided worrying findings for teachers. For example, Metzler (1989) found that only 10–20 per cent of total lesson time could be accurately seen as contributing to learning objectives. Other studies (reported in Mawer, 1995) found that less than 15 per cent of lesson time related to work on tasks of an appropriate level of difficulty, whilst more than twice that figure was taken up with waiting to carry out a task. Silverman (1991, p. 356) concluded from his own research that: 'the amount of time students spend practising . . . at an appropriate or successful level is positively related to student achievement'.

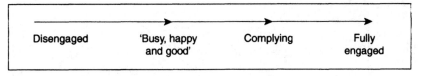

Figure 2.1   *Levels of engagement*

Some of the main obstacles to pupil participation, including queuing, too many users of limited equipment and too many players in a team, can be the result of inappropriate grouping. In particular, overly large groups of pupils engaged in an activity means that many of them will not have the opportunity to become fully involved, and this is most likely to be the case with less able pupils. Small-sided games and activities provide greater opportunities for all pupils to participate and achieve. An additional advantage of this approach is that teachers will be better able to differentiate the level of challenge for individual and group needs.

Things may not be as simple as they first appear. Certainly, it does seem to be the case that pupils are much less likely to learn if they are not participating in the lesson (at least, they are unlikely to learn things that the teacher wants them to). However, pupils who are complying with the teacher's instruction may still not be fully engaged with the content of a lesson in a meaningful way, and may not be benefiting from the learning experiences as well as they might. They could merely be going through the motions of a task, with little enthusiasm or interest: 'Student compliance alone is a very limited goal for an educational program. Student compliance suggests that the students are able to do what the teacher says – they are willing to co-operate with the teacher' (Rink, 1993, p. 128).

Compliance is certainly preferable to non-compliance or misbehaviour. It is also an improvement on the 'busy, happy and good' phenomenon, since complying pupils, at least, are participating in the planned activities of the lesson. However, a worthy goal of any teaching is to reach a stage where pupils take responsibility for their own learning (see Figure 2.1). Full engagement in a task suggests that pupils are so involved that they are able to operate with minimal direction or monitoring by the teacher.

Pupils who are fully engaged in their work have the greatest potential for learning and achievement. They enter into a virtuous circle in which their initial motivation to learn and succeed leads to fuller engagement in tasks, which results in greater success, which

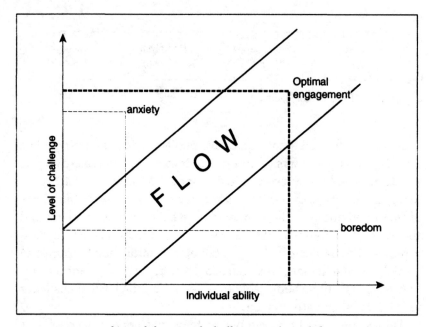

Figure 2.2 *Matching abilities and challenges* (adapted from Csikszentmihalyi, 1975)

inspires even greater motivation, and so on. At the same time they are also learning valuable lessons for life. Outside of prison and hospital, most adults do not receive anything like the level of supervision that pupils experience at school. Self-responsibility, therefore, is an important and necessary ability to acquire. It is part of what is now commonly referred to as the citizenship curriculum, and physical education provides a particularly powerful medium for this sort of learning.

Beyond Boredom and Anxiety

An interesting approach to the psychology of motivation is provided by Csikszentmihalyi (1975). In considering optimal motivation in different domains, he came to the conclusion that motivation was highest when the challenge posed by an activity was matched by the individual's personal abilities and skills (see Figure 2.2). Csikszentmihalyi described this state as 'flow', or supreme engagement in a task.

Matching challenge to ability is of great importance in this model, and mismatch can result in anxiety (if the challenge exceeds ability) or boredom (if ability is greater than the challenge). According to this model, assessment and monitoring of performance is key, and

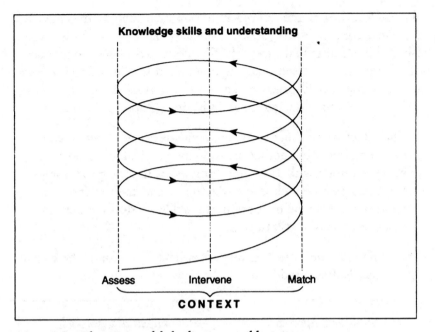

Figure 2.3 *The AIM model: facilitating pupil learning*

the teacher needs to continually observe and, if necessary reset tasks, to ensure optimal engagement.

One way of facilitating a successful convergence of challenge and ability is to view teaching as a process of assessment, intervention and matching:

Assess – observe and monitor pupil performance;
Intervene – correct errors, introduce new skills or change practice;
Match – adapt the level of challenge to better meet individual or group needs.

According to this AIM model, the process of teaching and learning is a continuous one: once the activity has been adapted in an attempt to better converge with pupils' abilities, the teacher reassesses the accuracy of the match, intervenes if appropriate, and so on. If the teacher is successful in matching ability to challenge, pupils' learning and performance should improve, and so the process of assess, intervene and match becomes a 'virtuous cycle', as the learner works at increasingly higher levels (see Figure 2.3).

Conversely, if the teacher fails to match ability and challenge, pupils can become frustrated or apprehensive, and enter into a 'vicious cycle', whereby their performance or behaviour deteriorates.

How would this operate in practice? A natural complement to

the AIM model is the approach to games teaching advocated by Macfadyen and Osborne (2000) and Bailey (2000b), which might be labelled the 'contextual approach'. They offer a challenge to the 'standard' approach to lesson planning in which it is assumed that formal skill learning should precede games playing (Gallahue, 1993; Bott, 1997). In contrast, Macfadyen and Osborne (2000, p. 144) argue:

> The effective teaching of games is analogous to effective strategies employed in another areas of the curriculum. That is, to provide pupils with the opportunities to have a go at something, assess how well they are doing it and then to intervene appropriately to help develop the skills, understandings and strategies involved still further.

The difference in structuring games lessons within these two approaches is illustrated below:

'Standard' approach	'Contextual' approach
Introduction	Introduction
⇓	⇓
Skill learning	**Game**
⇓	⇓
Game	**Skill learning**
⇓	⇓
Conclusion	**Game**
	⇓
	Conclusion

The standard approach assumes that pupils will understand when, how and why to use the skills they are learning. However, evidence suggests that this need not be the case, even when teachers clearly explain the application of a skill (Bransford et al., 1999). Evidence from the psychology of learning shows the enormous importance of *context* in skill learning (Lave, 1988): learning experiences are more effective when they reflect the specific situations in which they are intended to be used. It seems logical, therefore, that the best way to learn to play a particular game is within the context of that game. So, rather than beginning with isolated skills and techniques, it seems preferable to start with a well-selected small-sided game, and inter-

vene with skills and techniques once the learners have some understanding of the context in which they would be applied.

It is important to stress that this approach is not a rejection of the
importance of skill learning in physical education. On the contrary,
skill learning lies at its heart. However, it is stressed that learning is
more likely to occur and be maintained if it is perceived by the
learner to be meaningful and relevant to their needs. The contextual
model outlined above need not result in any reduction in skills
learning. It merely prefaces the learning and practice of these skills
with a clearer picture of the activities in which they are to be
applied.

Positively Purposeful Learning

As was discussed in Chapter 1, the educational goals of physical
education are much broader than those associated with physical
skills and competences. We can distinguish between educational
values that focus on the *content* of lessons – the skills, knowledge and
understanding fostered – and those that emphasize the *context* within
which these lessons take place – the opportunities for personal
achievement, social learning and self-responsibility. Both content
and context give physical education its distinctive character and
account for its particular contribution to the educational development of children. Just as teachers offer opportunities for pupils to
develop their physical and intellectual skills and techniques, they
should also strive to develop pupils' self-management and self-
responsibility.

Teachers have a vital role to play in encouraging, fostering and
refining these capabilities. There is considerable evidence that teaching styles can support the development of self-responsibility in pupils
(this is discussed in detail in Chapter 4). Another widely cited
approach is Hellison's 'Responsibility Model' (Hellison and Templin,
1991). Hellison hypothesized a series of levels and sublevels (see
Figure 2.4), each reflecting goals towards which individuals aim to
progress. There is no contention that these levels represent developmental stages through which children move. Instead, they articulate
the kinds of responsibilities that pupils need to consider in everyday
contexts:

> This educational process is intended to cause students to *feel*
> empowered and purposeful, to experience making responsible
> commitments to themselves and others, to strive to develop
> themselves despite external force, to be willing to risk popular-

Levels

Level 1 – Self-control and respect for the rights and feelings of others

- Self-control

- Inclusion

- Negotiating conflicts

- Internalizing respect

Level 2 – Participation and effort

- Going through the motions

- Exploring effort

- Redefining success

Level 3 – Self-direction

- Independence

- Goal-setting

- Knowledge base

- Plan and evaluate

Level 4 – Caring and helping

- Supporting others

- Helping others

- Group welfare

Strategies

Awareness

Experience

Choice

Problem-solving/student sharing

Self-reflection

Counselling time

Teaching qualities

Figure 2.4   *The 'Responsibility Model'*

ity to live by a set of principles, to understand their essential relatedness to others, and to distinguish between their own personal preferences and activities that impinge on their rights and welfare of others. (Hellison and Templin, 1991, p. 104)

These goals are shared and discussed with pupils, to offer a common vocabulary for the teacher and pupils. Moreover, strategies are suggested that can help pupils become more aware of experience, make decisions about and reflect on their goals and responsibilities: 'The model requires a conceptualisation of the teaching act that is different from more traditional models. If students are to become responsible, they must experience some responsibility' (Hellison and Templin, 1991, p. 108).

Motivation and Learning

Whatever the final formula for success for Physical Education over the future years, it is clear that an understanding of the psychology of motivation, with particular reference to the physical environment, could (a) help Physical Educators improve the quality of their interaction with students and (b) help in designing programmes which work to promote activity. (Fox, 1988, p. 34)

It is a matter of common sense that motivation plays a role of central importance in learning. Even the most technically skilled teacher has little chance of maximizing learning if pupils lack effort, enthusiasm or interest during lessons. Not unsurprisingly, theorists have been very interested in exploring psychological theories of motivation and their implications for physical education (cf. Vanden Auweele *et al.*, 1999 for a useful overview).

Pupils in physical education classes are required to experience activities of different types and of varying degrees of difficulty. According to Papaioannou and Goudas (1999, p. 53), pupils often pose two basic questions to themselves when approaching tasks:

1. Can I do it?
2. Do I want to do it?

The first question is about competence or ability to perform the task. The second question is concerned with its interest or value. The way that pupils address these two questions has important implications for their motivation.

A number of studies have suggested that two orientations on learners' goals can influence learners' behaviour and work in the school environment (Nicholls, 1984; Sarrazin and Famose, 1999; Roberts, 1992). A *mastery perspective* (sometimes called a task orientation) arises when a learner focuses on demonstrating ability or competence at a task, and where the emphasis is on self-improvement or self-comparison. A *competitive perspective* (or ego orientation), on the other hand, is characterized by a learner seeking to compare ability or performance with others.

A common assumption seems to be that the competitive perspective is the norm for children, especially within the context of physical education. However, research suggests that this is not necessarily the case. Whilst teenagers often exhibited a competitive goal orientation, younger children seem to be far more influenced by mastery goals (as well as social approval) than competition (Roberts and Treasure, 1993). Although boys are generally more competitive than girls, younger children of both sexes tend to be more concerned with the improvement of skills and overall development of physical competence than being favourably compared with their peers.

Some writers have suggested that the 'motivational climate' created by teachers can have a powerful effect on the way children perceive a task (Ames and Archer, 1988; Roberts, 1992). Teachers' responses to a pupil's activity can initially conflict with and then begin to guide the learner's assessment of the situation. Moreover, there is evidence that pupils are able to pick up cues from the way their teachers present lessons, and the elements that are emphasized and rewarded (Papaioannou and Goudas, 1999). By giving certain cues, and making explicit expectations, teachers can structure the learning climate so that task- or ego-involved conceptions of ability are the criteria by which performance is evaluated (Ames and Archer, 1988). A competitive orientation is most likely to be fostered when pupils are compared with each other or against some pre-existing criteria, or when led to question their own ability. By contrast, mastery orientation is more likely be to generated when activities either stress the learning process and personal development or when they foster a greater sense of control by the learners (Sarrazin and Famose, 1999; see Chapter 4).

This idea of a motivational climate deserves serious attention by physical educators, particularly as it relates to the behaviour of pupils in their lessons. Children who have adopted a mastery orientation seem to be better able to select challenging tasks, persist despite set-backs and remain interested in the activity. They also seem better able to develop positive relationships with peers. Some of this may also be true of learners with a competitive perspective, but evidence does suggest that there are greater risks of problematic behaviours emerging. Pupils with high perceptions of their own ability often exhibit the same qualities as learners focusing on mastery. However, pupils with low perceptions of ability tend to exhibit behaviour characterized by poor motivation, avoidance of challenge and lacking in persistence (Hayward, 1993). The negative reaction to competitive situations may be more apparent in girls than in boys (Sports Council, 1993). Also, learners' competitive frames can be very fragile, and confidence in their own abilities can be damaged by failure or frustration (Dweck, 1986). Whatever the perceived ability, learners with a competitive orientation to their participation tend to be the ones most likely to give up sport as they move through and leave school (Roberts and Treasure, 1993).

It needs to be stressed that the previous discussion is not a condemnation of competition itself. On the contrary, it is fully accepted that competitive experiences make a distinctive and important contribution to physical education. Moreover, many pupils greatly enjoy the competitive aspects of the subject. The point is one of emphasis. Competition can create the context of participation, but there are dangers associated with making it the goal of participation in physical education (Bailey, 1999b). An excessive emphasis upon winning can, in the long-run, lead to a rejection of the whole enterprise of physical activity. Ironically, by emphasizing the importance of doing one's best, trying to beat previous performances and improving skills, the teacher facilitates greater enjoyment of the competitive elements (when they are present and appropriate) in the physical education lesson.

Positive Class Management

Maintaining control during lessons is probably the paramount cause for concern among inexperienced teachers. Mawer's study (1995) found that 60 per cent of heads of physical education departments questioned rated discipline and control as being the major difficulties experienced by those new to the profession. At the same time, effective control is one of the most fundamental skills to develop as a teacher, since its absence makes safe, effective learning virtually impossible.

There is a close and intrinsic link between control strategies and positive teaching: the best control is preventative; it stops or minimizes problems before they arise through general good practice in teaching. Teachers who plan their lessons well and deliver lessons that are properly organized are also those who maintain the most order, presumably because their minds are freer during lessons to observe pupils' performance and behaviour, rather than worry about the next stage of the lesson. This seems to be particularly the case in physical education: most pupils want to achieve and co-operate nearly all of the time, and they are supportive of teachers who try to help them learn.

Bailey (2001a) has summarized the research and guidance to teachers on establishing positive control through preventative, positive strategies. The main principles are listed below:

- Maintain a positive, purposeful working environment.
- Establish effective class management and organization systems.
- Implement a workable, shared set of rules and routines.
- Plan and deliver challenging and rewarding activities.
- Make sure pupils understand the reasons why they are doing the activities.
- Encourage high standards and value pupils' effort and performance.
- Plan for and teach in recognition of individual needs and differences.
- Be clear in articulating and sharing expectations with pupils.
- Be firm and fair.
- Develop positive supportive relationships with pupils.
- Organize time and space to facilitate maximum learning and participation.

(See Lambirth and Bailey, 2000 and Mawer, 1995, for detailed guidance on teaching skills and class management strategies for physical education.)

Thinking About Misbehaviour

Thorough planning, effective class management strategies and well-developed teaching skills can make a significant contribution to class control. However, acts of misconduct and misbehaviour may still arise in even the best lessons: 'Discipline is what you do when, despite your best efforts, students do not co-operate and choose to behave in inappropriate ways' (Rink, 1993, p. 140).

Serious misbehaviour in lessons is quite rare. The Elton Report on *Discipline in Schools* (DES/WO, 1989) found that the most troublesome behaviour for teachers was usually not serious misconduct, but rather mild, irritating disturbance, such as talking out of turn, interfering with the work of others and work avoidance. This is supported by Wragg's (1993) observational study of Primary classrooms, where only 2 per cent of the deviant behaviour observed fell outside of the classification 'mild'. However, Wragg also found that these mild acts occurred very frequently (in about half of the lessons observed), and were most common when boys worked together. Similar results were found within the context of physical education by Hardy (1999), who found that the most frequently occurring types of misbehaviour during lessons were (in descending order):

1. Not paying attention during the teacher's instructions.
2. Not carrying out the teacher's instructions.

3. Disrupting others.
4. Refusing to take part in the lesson.
5. Not carrying out the rules and procedure.
6. Wishing to be the centre of attention.

It can be difficult to identify precisely the causes of such behaviour. Of course, some misbehaviour is simply an expression of immaturity; children behave in childish ways. It is also worth bearing in mind the comment of a newly qualified teacher (cited by Mawer 1995, p. 126): 'You have 20–30 people bringing their own personal baggage with them to a lesson. There is no doubt that they will have varied experiences and intentions.' It is also worth acknowledging that there can be certain pay-offs for misbehaving pupils. Robertson (1989) stresses that pupils can receive benefits from misbehaving, such as gaining attention, avoiding work or simply excitement. In such circumstance, teachers responding to the challenge may be unwittingly encouraging the very behaviours they seek to stop.

Of course, the teacher can, directly or indirectly, be the cause of misbehaviour in pupils, due to inappropriate teaching. Bailey (2001a) lists some of the main teacher-initiated causes of misbehaviour:

- Instructions are not presented clearly.
- Equipment is not readily available.
- The teacher arrives after the pupils have started to arrive.
- Pupils feel that the teacher is unfair, or treats some pupils preferentially.
- Pupils are bored with an activity.
- Pupils are unable to perform the activity.
- Pupils cannot see the point of the task.
- Transitions between activities are not smooth and well organized.
- The teacher needlessly interrupts pupils during the task.
- The teacher spends too much time talking or introducing an activity.
- Pupils spend too much time queuing or waiting.
- Groups are too large for maximum participation and activity.
- The teacher stands in an inappropriate place.

Some pupils turn up to the lesson already socially or emotionally disturbed, and this can impact upon the way they behave. The main patterns of such disruptive behaviour include:

- Boredom
- Anxiety
- Antipathy
- Social dominance
- Social isolation.

Enjoyment and fun are important parts of the frame of reference for pupils in physical education and physical activity (Goudas and Biddle, 1994), and teachers spend a considerable amount of time trying to make lessons as enjoyable as possible. Motivation, it has been argued, is a vital factor in learning and engagement, and pupil enjoyment of an activity relates very strongly to this motivation. Conversely, *boredom* is a barrier to learning as it leads pupils to disengage from learning and participation, and pupils are much more likely to misbehave when they disengage from their work. Laws and Fisher (1999) found that pupils tend to find it difficult to express the meanings they attach to concepts like fun or enjoyment: 'PE is fun because it's fun . . . it's the experience of it . . . because what you do is fun in PE' (Year 7 pupil cited in Laws and Fisher, 1999, p. 26). The same pupil was more clear about negative aspects of physical education experience: 'standing around in the cold . . . or getting told off . . . and when the lessons aren't good . . . when the teachers don't make it fun or enjoyable . . . it's boring then.'

Similarly, pupils who approach activities with *anxiety* are more likely to behave in inappropriate ways than others, if only in the hope of avoiding taking part. Physical education provides a number of opportunities for pupils to be adventurous or to test their limits, and these experiences can incite fear or anxiety in some pupils: 'One pupil's challenge can easily become another's fear' (Bailey, 2001a, p. 106). Even less overtly adventurous tasks within the physical education curriculum may cause anxiety for some pupils owing to the uniquely public nature of much of the participation and performance.

Pupils have feelings of *antipathy* towards physical education when they decide that the subject is of little relevance or value to them. Whilst physical education is consistently rated as among the most worthwhile and popular of subjects in the curriculum by pupils (Birtwistle and Brodie, 1991), some pupils do develop a progressive disillusionment with physical education, especially as they move towards the end of their secondary schooling. Criticisms have centred on perceptions that pupils only experience a narrow range of (predominantly male-orientated) activities, that these activities are often presented in an over-competitive form, and that there is a mismatch between the physical education curriculum and the sorts of physical activities that young people are likely to experience once they leave school. This problem is particularly apparent among girls as they move towards the end of their secondary schooling, who sometimes dismiss physical education as 'unfeminine, irrelevant and childish' (Kay, 1995, p. 59). Feelings of antipathy towards a subject mean that pupils are prone towards misbehaviour or lesson avoidance (e.g., 15- and 16-year-old girls are twice as likely to miss physical education lessons as boys (Milosevic, 1996)). Significantly, in this light, Fernandez-Balboa (1991) found that the main cause of misconduct in physical education lessons was 'boredom'.

Saunders (cited in Cohen *et al.*, 1996, p. 303) views *social dominance* as an extension of the problem of antipathy:

> Some physically and socially mature pupils seem to have a need for frequent reinforcement in the form of attention from their peers. This is often achieved at school by challenging the authority of the teacher. If the challenge is not met it can be taken up by other pupils and the lesson ruined, and as a result the assertion of the teacher's authority becomes difficult in future lessons.

Some feminist writers have accused male members of the physical education profession of exacerbating this problem through their own assertion of their masculinity (Flintoff, 1998). Teachers who continually seek to demonstrate their physical prowess create a challenge to which some socially ambitious pupils might seek to rise, or they may simply legitimize such behaviours in other pupils in the school. It is very difficult for physical education teachers to condemn or punish acts of bullying when their own behaviours are sometimes interpreted as acts of bullying by certain pupils in the school.

Physical competence is a major factor influencing social acceptance in children of all ages and both sexes (Bailey, 1999b). Some pupils may find themselves at the periphery of social groups, as they do not possess the necessary physical abilities to be accepted by their peers. One way some children deal with this problem is to try to win favour with peers through a different means, such as acting out an extreme form of a group's behaviour. Another response to the pressure of *social isolation* is to increase the degree of alienation from the main group by behaving in a malicious way to peers, or by disengaging from activities that are generally valued, such as physical education.

Understanding the reasons for misbehaviour can help the teacher respond in an appropriate manner to an incident. Problems of this sort are often best addressed by speaking with pupils, and attempting to ascertain the specific root of the difficulty. It may be that the teacher's behaviour in a certain situation is the real problem, or that the problem lies with the way the curriculum is structured and presented to pupils. In both cases, chastizing pupils will probably only result in a short-term change of pupil behaviour, as the underlying cause remains. On other occasions, though, the cause of misconduct may lie with the pupils, and the teacher needs to consider the most effective way of responding.

Managing Misbehaviour

As discussed above the great majority of incidents of misbehaviour are rather mild, and do not constitute a direct challenge to a teacher's authority. The apparent triviality of such events does not mean that teachers should avoid them, however. On the contrary, deliberately ignoring acts of misconduct can be misconstrued by pupils as either weakness or ignorance (Cohen et al., 1996).

Bailey (2001a) coined the phrase 'proto-misbehaviour' to refer to apparently trivial acts of misbehaviour that may, if not addressed by the teacher, develop into more serious disciplinary problems. Overreacting to a minor problem like chatting or avoiding work can actually lead to that problem worsening, since the teacher's response can be seen as unreasonable or unfair. It can also mean that everyone else in the vicinity of the incident is disturbed and their learning halted. In physical education, which usually takes place in a very large space, this can be a particular problem. Minor acts of misconduct of this kind are best dealt with in a positive and constructive manner, perhaps through the use of non-verbal communication or class management strategies (see Table 2.1), or by responding to them as they would an incorrect answer or performance (Rink, 1993).

There are times, however, when approaches of this sort do not have the desired effect, and misbehaviour continues. Simply repeating the failed strategy is unlikely to succeed, and can indicate that the teacher is struggling to deal with a problem.

Reprimands can prove to be a useful response to repeated misconduct. Their effectiveness is judged by the extent to which they prevent further misbehaviour, and return pupils to engagement in their learning tasks. The most effective forms of reprimand are brief, clear and direct regarding the unacceptable behaviour, and accom-

Strategy	Application
Scanning the area	The teacher should consciously scan the area to ensure all pupils are engaged in the planned task; potential problems might be spotted and addressed; pupils noting this attention are less inclined to deviate from the activity.
Eye contact	Eye contact shows that teachers are aware of behaviour without disturbing others; can be accompanied by stopping talking or changes of body language.
Proximity control	Moving physically closer to misbehaving pupils shows the teacher's awareness; can lead to a 'ripple effect', as peers become aware of the teacher's attention.
Desist	Simply asking pupils to stop their misbehaviour can be effective, if not over-used or repeated for the same pupil; can be rephrased into a positive form, whereby the teacher suggests an alternative form of behaviour.
Questioning	Well-focused questions can remind pupils of the planned task, as well as show teacher's awareness of their behaviour.
Relocation	Moving an offender to a new space can remove the cause of the disturbance, as well as show teacher's disapproval.

Table 2.1   *Class management and non-verbal strategies for dealing with proto-misbehaviours*

panied by suggestions for alternative types of behaviour. Private reprimands, where the teacher takes the offender away from the rest of the class, can be particularly useful, but their application can be restricted by other events taking place in the area. Whatever form the reprimand takes, it is important to stress that it is the behaviour, not the person, that is being condemned. The desired outcome is a return to work, not a victory.

Punishment is usually a last resort. Its use arises when misbehaviour is deliberate, repeated, and has not been corrected by other strategies. A range of approaches is available, from temporarily withdrawing a pupil from a class, to exclusion from the school (DES/WO, 1989), and these are usually determined at a whole-school level. Punishment should not be used when it is apparent that the child is trying to improve their behaviour. Good and Brophy (1991) make the valid point that punishment can control misbehaviour, but by itself it will not teach desirable behaviours or even reduce the pupils' desire to misbehave. So punishment alone is a limited strategy, and ought to be accompanied by an attempt to understand and address the root cause of the misconduct.

Conclusion

This chapter has discussed the need for positive and purposeful learning environments for physical education. Research and common sense suggest that positive approaches to class management and control are more effective than negative ones: pupils are better motivated to learn, to behave and to fully engage with the physical education curriculum if they feel supported and valued. If their experiences of physical activities at school are positive, they are also more likely to continue to enjoy the health-promoting benefits of activity once they leave formal schooling.

There are no universal recipes for success; learners are individuals and they have distinctive ways of responding to situations and challenges. The effective teacher will be sensitive to these differences, and will react to the needs of the individual and the situation. The teacher who keeps pupils fully engaged in learning is likely to facilitate greater achievement, higher levels of motivation and less misbehaviour.

CHAPTER 3

Planning for Effective Learning

Introduction

Teaching is a complex activity requiring teachers to make a continuous series of decisions based upon the curriculum, the pupils and the match between the two. Effective planning is one way of supporting such teaching. There are different sorts of plans for different purposes. Plans can help the teacher prepare for the coming year, for the coming term or half-term, or the coming lesson. In all cases, planning is an essential ingredient in successful and rewarding teaching. This chapter examines the decisions teachers need to make when they plan, and identifies the elements of effective planning in physical education.

Planning and Pupil Learning

There is little doubt that effective teacher planning is one of the most significant factors affecting pupil learning. Whilst thorough planning by the teacher alone will not guarantee learning, it makes it considerably more likely. It provides the teacher with a safety net, offering support and guidance for the effective organization and delivery of lessons. In a largely practical subject like physical education, that is of great importance. It also offers a bridge between the aims and content of the curriculum and the activity that is taking place in a specific lesson.

Research suggests that planning is one of the most significant factors in teacher effectiveness and pupil learning. Teachers who plan their work in physical education (in comparison with those who do not) exhibit a number of important qualities associated with pupil learning, including:

- Greater use of equipment and facilities.
- More directions.
- More careful and precise organization of lessons.
- Clearer presentations.
- More specific feedback.
- Greater variety and better progression of activities.
- Better timing of lessons.
- Greater ability to analyse pupils' needs.
- Higher levels of activity and time 'on task' among pupils.
  (Adapted from Mawer, 1995)

In their review of the literature on teacher planning, Clark and Yinger (1987, p. 95) concluded that teacher planning 'does influence opportunities to learn, content coverage, grouping for instruction, and the general focus of classroom processes'.

Despite the agreement among researchers and writers that effective planning provides the foundation for pupil learning, trainee or inexperienced teachers sometimes bemoan the time and effort spent constructing their plans. They may point to more experienced colleagues who seem to deliver high quality lessons without detailed plans. Indeed, it can be easy to forget the wealth of knowledge and skills that some teachers have at their disposal. Such knowledge is not limited to a familiarity with various activities, techniques and rules, but to a myriad of less obvious aspects: leading the pupils into the physical education area; changing between tasks; arranging groups; spotting potential problems before they arise; and so on. It is a mistake, though, to conclude that because some experienced colleagues do not produce detailed lesson plans, that they are not planning, nor that planning is secondary to actual teaching.

Functions of Planning

There are a number of important functions of planning that support learning, some of which are discussed below.

Anne Williams (1996, p. 29) speaks of planning as '*articulation of thinking*'. In other words, careful planning provides an opportunity for the teacher to think through the lesson, in its entirety and in its parts, before delivering it. This process of thinking through aspects of the coming lesson is of great importance to the teacher, as Mawer

(1995, p. 54) makes clear: 'Teaching is a professional "thinking" activity and what is actually done is largely dependent upon the teacher's thought processes that have gone before the lesson.' Teachers need to be able to think on their feet, to deal with problems and changing circumstances as lessons progress. It is unreasonable to expect inexperienced teachers to address these matters, *as well* as think about more general issues of lesson content, presentation and organization. These are things better dealt with *before* the lesson begins. Planning allows the teacher to visualize the lesson, its activities, its structure, and how it is to be delivered. Writing a plan down can give an even clearer idea of how the different elements relate to each other, and to how well they address the objectives set. This is of no small benefit if one considers the wealth of questions that·lie implicitly within a plan, such as:

- How do I gain the pupils' attention and interest at the beginning?
- How do I best explain the theme?
- How are pupils to move from activity to activity safely and quickly?
- What teaching methods best suit the lesson objective?
- How do I organize pupils into groups for different tasks?
- How do I arrange the area, the equipment, the pupils?
- What vocabulary should I use?
- How do I calm the pupils down at the end of the lesson?

Physical education is a notoriously broad and wide-ranging subject. Not surprisingly, subject knowledge presents a major source of concern for many teachers (Mawer, 1995). Moreover, simply having a well-developed understanding of the divergent elements of the physical education curriculum is insufficient, as the effective teacher is one who can present the curriculum in a way that is meaningful to the pupils. Lesson planning can serve as a valuable *aide-memoire*, a summary of the key teaching points for a certain skill or the rules of a game. Once again, the act of preparing the plan will identify gaps in knowledge, and prompt reference to a textbook or guide. The information is then available to the teacher, should the need arise.

There are some times when the teacher may need to use plans more directly. For example, certain topics may be rather complex (such as some of the scientific content of GCSE and Advanced Level syllabi), or demand very accurate presentation to the class (such as rules to an unfamiliar game), and in these circumstances 'scripting of input' (Bailey, 2000b) may be appropriate. By summarizing the plan onto a small postcard that fits inside a pocket, the teacher can make sure that the key points are readily available. Another common direct use of plans in physical education lessons relates to the layout of apparatus or equipment. For example, setting up gymnastic apparatus can be a time-consuming activity, but this can be considerably reduced with the aid of a clear plan, especially when displayed for pupils to follow.

Planning can act as a *warning*. By offering an overview of the lesson ahead, it highlights necessary pre-lesson preparation of resources and possible sources of disturbance. Many potential problems can be identified *before* the lesson even starts: 'bottlenecks' in setting up equipment; changing between activities; and so on. Planning offers the teacher the chance to think about the best ways of dealing with these issues in advance, and, hopefully, of avoiding them. Therefore a sound lesson plan also forms part of an effective risk-assessment exercise, which is imperative for all lessons: safe teaching underpins pupil learning.

Finally, plans provide a useful record of the teaching and the intended learning that has taken place. It is very often important to have written evidence of work carried out, such as during teacher training or an inspection. As such, planning is a relatively simple, concrete means of showing that adequate care and attention has been taken in preparation of lessons. Less ominously, written plans provide valuable sources for future lesson ideas, as well as a basis from which later work can be developed.

Planning Decisions

In planning, the teacher considers a number of related issues that determine the character of the lessons. One way of conceptualizing this is as a series of variables relating to the organization, the presentation and the content of the lesson. Each relates to a different aspect of the overall lesson, but they are inextricably linked together (see Figure 3.1).

By making decisions about the different elements, both for the whole class and for individual pupils, the teacher begins to draw out a structure for his or her planning. Moreover, as will be seen a little later, a model of this sort provides a useful starting point for differentiating to meet the needs of individual pupils.

Organization refers to the social context of the teaching. Planning for organization ranges from relatively broad issues related to the character of pupil interaction – co-operative, competitive, individu-

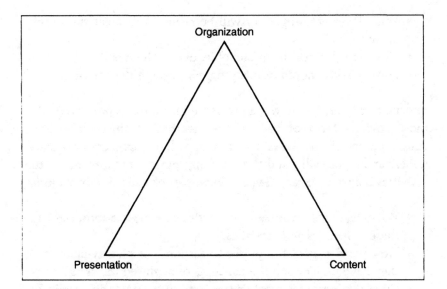

Figure 3.1   *Main variables in planning physical education lessons*

alistic – to more specific questions like the size of groups and the arrangement of pupils around an area. As the teacher considers organizational variables, it is worth considering:

- Should the pupils be grouped or work individually?
- How shall I group the pupils?
- How shall we use the physical education area?
- How much pupil interaction is relevant?
- What are the different roles that pupils need to take?
- What is the appropriate behaviour and conduct for these activities?

Content refers to the identification of knowledge, understanding, attitudes and skills that the teacher aims to develop. In many cases, some of these questions will have been answered for the teacher some way in advance of planning, such as in the National Curriculum (DfEE/QCA, 1999). Nonetheless, this does not remove the teacher's role in determining the aspects of the curriculum to be focused upon and the way in which this is to take place. In planning for content, the teacher is answering a series of fundamental questions:

- What do I want to achieve by the end of the lesson / scheme of work?
- What activities will facilitate success of these objectives?

- What level of complexity will be required to meet the pupils' needs?
- How do I progress from one objective to the next?
- How quickly should pupils progress through the activities?

Presentation refers to the way in which information is presented. The most obvious form of presentation is that of the teacher, but consideration of the ways the pupils will be expected to show understanding or skills, and the most appropriate equipment for the activities is also necessary. Typical examples of issues might include:

- What teaching strategies and styles are most appropriate for these objectives and activities?
- How will I expect the pupils to respond, or give evidence that they have understood the concepts or acquired the skills?
- What equipment is most appropriate to support this activity?
- How shall I organize my time during the lesson?
- Will I require other adults?
- Who will demonstrate?

Thinking teaching through in this way at the planning stage can help reduce the anxiety and uncertainty that are natural responses during the early phases of a teacher's career or when the teacher is faced with a new, unfamiliar activity. Teachers who have planned thoroughly do not have to worry about every detail of the content, organization and presentation at the time of delivery. In this way, they will be much better able to deal with those unexpected concerns that may arise during the lesson. Such thorough preparation can only serve to boost the teacher's confidence and free the mind of unnecessary 'baggage' and anxiety so that it is possible to concentrate on other aspects of the lesson. Of particular importance will be more opportunities to analyse pupils' actions and adjust the tasks set accordingly to maximize pupil learning.

Levels of Planning

Planning is an indication of a teacher's intention. It can indicate the teacher's intentions for pupils' learning and activity during the coming lesson, or the coming year. Clark and Yinger (1987, p. 87) suggest that teachers' planning is a 'nested process'. For example, specific tasks are 'nested' within individual lessons, which, in turn, are 'nested' within daily plans, and these within weekly, termly and yearly plans. Teachers need to plan for each of these levels, from the

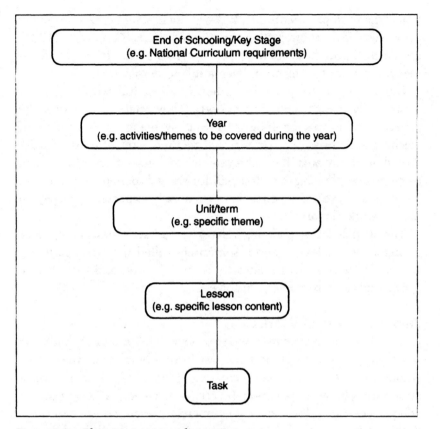

Figure 3.2   *Planning as a nested process*

highly specific and immediate to the general and distant, and they need to understand how each level relates to the other.

There are a number of ways of thinking about this nested process. For example, the School Curriculum and Assessment Authority (SCAA, 1995) identifies three levels of planning: long-term, medium-term and short-term. A related model is presented in Figure 3.2, which aims to reflect the different levels of planning decisions made by teachers in their everyday work.

There are certain curriculum expectations that relate to expected pupil learning at the end of their school career or Key Stage. In the United Kingdom, these expectations are determined, to a large extent, by central government and its associated agencies. The National Curriculum, for example, indicates End of Key Stage Descriptions, and these direct schools' and physical education departments' long-term plans and aims. However, because these expectations may relate to performance or understanding in future years, many departments break down such statements into yearly plans and aims. An interesting variation on this is Siedentop's (1994) notion of 'Sport Education' which operates at the level of *seasons* that can run for two terms or even a full academic year.

Units of work are plans for either a half or full-term's work (or occasionally a slightly shorter period). They relate to the activities expected of a specific group, as well as being an indication of teaching and assessment strategies. Together, a set of units of work should lead towards the achievement of longer-term aims. Such *medium-term planning* is a vital skill for the inexperienced teacher to develop, and even trainee teachers are usually expected to engage in unit-of-work planning.

The final level of planning relates to the activities taking place during a specific lesson, and is sometimes called *short-term planning*. A series of lesson plans relates to a unit of work, and they can be considered as more immediate stages.

Planning Units of Work

A unit of work represents a series of lessons with a class, based on some topic or theme. A unit can last from a number of weeks to a whole term. In many ways, creating units of work is the most important phase of planning (Clark and Yinger, 1987), because effective teaching does not involve merely presenting isolated tasks. Rather, it is concerned with a systematic progression through knowledge, understanding and skills. Planning at the level of units (as well as lessons) leads the teacher to have an awareness of the bigger picture of pupil learning: how do specific tasks and lessons relate to the longer-term learning of the class. Once the teacher is able to think through the overall objectives of the unit, the progression of activities and the necessary preparation, lesson planning becomes a relatively simple process of adding a level of greater detail and guidance onto teaching approaches.

Figures 3.3 and 3.4 (following) offer two examples of approaches to unit planning. Figure 3.3 is adapted from early guidance for the English and Welsh National Curriculum (NCC, 1992), and provides a lesson-by-lesson outline of the work to be covered during the unit. The second, adapted from Bailey (2000b) offers a more flexible model (see also Bott, 1997, and Bunker, 1994, for further approaches; cf. Bailey, 2001a for more information on the specific content of units of work).

Of vital importance in this process is an awareness of pupils' previous experience or knowledge of a particular area. If teachers are

	Lesson 1	Lesson 2	Lesson 3	Lesson 4	Lesson 5	Lesson 6
Theme						
Age of pupils						
Unit learning objectives						
Children with SEN/medical conditions						
Wider curricula opportunities (ICT; Citizenship; Literacy; Numeracy; SMSC)						
Duration of lesson						
Prior learning and experience of theme						
Lesson structure						
Lesson objectives						
Introduction Development Conclusion						
Resource/ Preparation						
Statutory requirements	Assessment criteria					

Figure 3.3   *An example of a lesson-by-lesson framework for a unit of work*

Theme	Age of pupils
	Duration/hours
Unit learning objectives	Attainment target references

| SEN/Medical conditions | Prior learning |

Learing activities (including differentiation)	Assessment (relate to learning objectives)	Resource/ preparation

Figure 3.4 *A flexible framework for a unit of work*

unable to ascertain information of this sort, they will need to consider simple assessment procedures at the beginning of the scheme (see Chapter 5).

In order to develop pupils' knowledge, skills and understanding, units usually focus upon a specific aspect of the physical education curriculum. Depending upon the age and experience of the pupils, skills, activities or themes may be taken as the units of work's focus. Of course, this distinction is rather simplistic, as there is a great deal of overlap. Nonetheless, it offers a convenient way of conceptualizing themes for units. Sample unit titles based upon each of these approaches are offered below:

Skills	athletics	high jump, relay, shot put
	games	passing, goal-keeping, batting
	gymnastics	vaulting, rolling, counter-balance
	swimming	stroke development, life-saving
Activities	games	football, cricket, netball
	dance	folk dance, jazz dance
	outdoor activities	climbing, hill-walking, canoeing
Themes	games	attack and defence, tactics
	gymnastics	symmetry/asymmetry, partner work, shape
	dance	the body, poems and stories

Planning for Progression

It is relatively easy for teachers to build up over time a collection of enjoyable and worthwhile activities for their physical education lessons. It is more difficult to use these tasks to develop pupils' skills and understanding through a progressive scheme. Indeed, the National Curriculum Council (NCC, 1992, unpaged) describes this aspect of planning as 'one of the biggest problems that faces teachers'. Progression is facilitated by planning with units of work, where it is possible to locate individual activities within a larger scheme and to trace the progression of associated skills.

Siedentop (1991) has suggested that a useful way of planning a unit of work is by *working backwards* from the final desired outcome to where the unit begins. In other words, the teacher needs to ask, 'Where do I wish the pupils to reach by the end of the unit?' And then, 'What is the best way to get them there?'

One way of conceptualizing progression is in terms of *continuing* and *blocked* elements (SCAA, 1995). Continuing work is that which requires regular reinforcement and development. In other words, continuing work refers to those activities that need regular teaching and consolidation, and often consists of those skills and concepts that comprise the 'basics' of an activity. A few examples of suitable themes for continuing work in physical education are:

- Movement into space in invasion games.
- Balance on body parts in gymnastics.
- Stroke development in swimming.

These are all activities to which the teacher needs to return again and again, at increasingly challenging levels, if skills and understanding are to develop.

Blocked work refers to a distinct body of skills or knowledge. Activities of this sort are usually relatively simple, and can be taught within a unit. They are often those subjects that pupils just need to know if they are to progress in an activity. Examples of blocked themes are:

- The off-side rule in football.
- The technique for taking one's own pulse during physical activity.
- Rules and routines for safe practice in the swimming pool.

Progression can also be enhanced by looking for links and associations between different units. SCAA (1995, p. 21) calls this linking of units '*curriculum coherence*', as the teacher or group of teachers aim to present the curriculum as a series of related pieces of work, not simply as a loose collection of activities. A useful way of contributing to curriculum coherence is to identify common aspects of shared skills or complimentary knowledge between units, and to draw upon these similarities to consolidate and broaden understanding in both units.

Taking games as an example, the common classification groups of striking/fielding, net/wall and invasion games each share a host of common demands and skills (see Read and Edwards, 1992, and Macfadyen and Osborne, 2000, for more guidance on this approach). Therefore, a unit of work focusing on tennis, for example, is likely

Tennis	Hitting ball into opponent's playing space to score or disadvantage opponent
Badminton	Playing ball with accuracy and control, using suitable pace and flight
Volleyball	Being well positioned and maintaining a strong ready stance; disguising shots
Squash	Predicting opponent's actions on the court

Table 3.1 *Shared demands and skills of net/wall games*

to raise issues of relevance for badminton, volleyball and squash (see Table 3.1).

An alternative approach is to think of progression in terms of the *qualities* that are being progressed. Williams (1996, p. 41) states that progression can be seen in the difficulty of the tasks achieved, in the quality of the response and in the context in which it is reproduced. By conceiving of planning in terms of progression, the teacher is encouraged to emphasize the development and the extension of pupils' understanding and skills, and thus the acquisition of substantial educational goals.

Progress in difficulty occurs when pupils are required to perform increasingly complex or challenging tasks. There are many different ways of making tasks more difficult, including:

- Extending pupils' skills repertoire (e.g., introducing the vaulting actions in gymnastics; distinguishing between various soccer passes).
- Moving from single to combined actions (passing – passing and moving to space; roll – roll to balance – jump to roll to balance).
- Reducing the time or space to perform an activity (restricting the playing area; planning for quick decision-making).
- Offering fewer options (limiting the range of 'allowed' actions in a gymnastics sequence).
- Developing more abstract or strategic ideas (discussing moods and feelings in dance; considering defensive patterns during games play).

(See Chapter 7 for a full discussion of differentiation methods.)

Progress in quality can be seen as pupils exhibit increasingly more sophisticated or successful performance of acquired skills. This can take a number of forms, including:

- Better clarity or articulation or shape in gymnastics or dance.
- Improved co-ordination of ball skills.
- Better poise, grace or fluency in movement.
- More refined strokes in swimming.
- Better timing or positioning of strikes in cricket.

Progress in context refers to pupils' ability to integrate actions into increasingly complex situations, such as:

- Working with a partner and then in larger groups.
- Working co-operatively and helping peers.
- Taking more initiative and responsibility in planning, performing and evaluating tasks.
- Applying skills learned in one context to a related one.
- Understanding when and where not to use specific skills.

Planning Lessons

Generally speaking, the more time spent planning units of work, the easier it is to devise effective lesson plans. However, lesson plans still require a great deal of thought, especially for inexperienced teachers, at the start of a year or when the activity or theme is unfamiliar. Lesson plans provide detail about specific activities, short-term goals and teaching strategies. In this respect, then, they form a safety net for the teacher working with a particular class on a particular day.

Kyriacou (1991) states that there are four major elements involved in lesson planning:

- Deciding educational objectives.
- Selecting and scripting the lesson.
- Preparing the props to be used.
- Deciding how to monitor and assess pupils' progress (which is discussed in a separate chapter; see Chapter 5).

Deciding educational objectives

The objectives of a lesson highlight the knowledge, understanding, skills or attitudes the teacher expects the pupils to acquire or develop during the lesson. Generally speaking, objectives should refer to the learning or behaviour of pupils, rather than that of the teacher. They should also be reasonable: in order to gain a clear idea of pupils' progress, objectives need to indicate something the teacher expects the pupils to have achieved by the end of the lesson. Therefore, the teacher needs to break up the targets of a larger scheme of work into manageable elements. For example, a unit might have as its main objective the development of pupils' rugby skills. This is far too vague and ill-defined for a lesson objective. Depending upon the age and experience of the pupils, lesson objectives might refer to pupils' understanding of the obstruction rule, the improvement of pupils' use of space in attack and defence, or the ability to perform simple tackles.

Selecting and scripting the lesson

Although physical education lessons necessarily involve physical activity, activity itself is not enough. Simply keeping pupils occupied with amusing games fails to fulfil the educative role of the subject, which demands that pupils *learn* something. The selection of the most appropriate activities to support such learning can be a complex task, and requires the teacher to focus upon the overall objectives, and how a particular lesson can contribute to them. A central aspect of this process is breaking up a larger theme into distinct parts, and designing a progression through them so that they make coherent and intellectual sense to the pupils and support their learning. Physical educators can sometimes be quite poor at retaining coherence in activities, and too often pupils practise dry, meaningless drills which bear little or no resemblance to the theme of which they are supposed to be a part.

In planning the activities of a lesson, the teacher attempts to address the needs of the group being taught. Therefore, an awareness of the background knowledge and abilities in the class is of utmost importance. Previous experience of the group will give the teacher some notion of the level of difficulty, quantity and pace of activities necessary. At the same time, it is always a good idea to over-plan in the sense of having sufficient additional activities in case the original work turns out to be inappropriate or is completed quicker than expected. As was discussed in Chapter 2, balancing a task's challenge with pupils' abilities is difficult: planning that is too ambitious can lead to pupils becoming anxious or frustrated; planning that is too easy can result in boredom.

Preparing the props to be used

By its nature, physical education usually involves the use of a range of equipment, from dance music to swimming floats, cricket bats and balls to climbing equipment. It is essential that these resources are prepared and made available by the teacher before the lesson commences. Adequate preparation of equipment can make a great difference to levels of pupil activity and consequently learning

(Hellison and Templin, 1991). Poor preparation can result in wasted time, misbehaviour and accidents.

The first stage of preparing for a lesson might involve the identification and selection of equipment needed. The teacher should aim to match the equipment to the needs of the pupils. *How old are the pupils? Do any have special needs that necessitate adapted resources? What are the previous experiences of the pupils?* The teacher also needs to ensure that there is enough equipment for the class being taught: in most cases, small groups or individual work is the norm.

Placement of equipment is an important issue and an under-acknowledged skill. The teacher who leaves the balls in the storage cupboard and then asks all of the pupils to 'get a ball each' is the teacher planning for disaster! This potential problem can be easily overcome by making equipment accessible to pupils, perhaps by placing it in a number of spots around the working area.

The Structure of the Lesson

The 'traditional model to lesson planning' (Bott, 1997; Mawer, 1995; Gallahue, 1993), offers one way forward:

1) Introduction

At the start of the lesson, the teacher needs to.

- Gain the pupils' attention.
- Introduce the theme of the day's lesson.
- Possibly review related work from previous lessons.
- Physically prepare the pupils for movement.

The warm-up phase of the lesson is of enormous importance, and should never be omitted. It should involve gentle *aerobic* activity that steadily raises the heart and breathing rate and warms the muscles and tendons. The easiest way to ensure that the appropriate muscles are prepared for action, and that the pupils are psychologically prepared for the content to follow, is to make the warm-up resemble the main theme. By warming up in context, pupils can also be introduced to a new skill/reinforce learning from a previous lesson. Planning in this way is clearly an efficient use of time.

2) Skill development

In this section of the lesson, pupils practise specific skills associated with an activity. In dance, for example, pupils might practise certain dance actions; in gymnastics they might perform a number of basic actions.

3) Climax
During this section of the lesson, pupils have the opportunity to apply the skills they have been learning or developing. This could be a dance, utilizing the various skills that have been practised, or a gymnastics sequence on apparatus, or a game.

4) Conclusion
The conclusion phase of a lesson is often forgotten in physical education, and this can lead to a number of problems. During the final phase of the lesson, pupils are both cooled down and calmed down by doing gentle, rhythmic exercise. The calming down element is often overlooked, but deserves consideration, particularly with younger pupils who can become very excited during the lesson, and need to be 'brought back to earth'. Furthermore, recapping on the key points helps to reinforce the lesson content, question the pupils on their understanding (to help the teacher reflect on the lesson's effectiveness), and set the next lesson in context.

Other Important Features of Lesson Planning

Teaching points
As well as a description of the different activities that pupils will be carrying out, lesson plans need to include explicit teaching points, which highlight important details related to the way activities are presented and the way in which they are carried out:

- What are the key points of a new skill?
- What qualities of movement or technical details will the teacher be looking for?
- Are there any particular safety issues that need to be observed during an activity?
- Are there specific words or concepts that need to be introduced?

Questions of this sort help the teacher ensure that the lesson promotes safe and worthwhile learning, rather than just activity.

Transitions
It is in the periods of transition between one activity and another that many problems of misbehaviour or safety occur. An instruction to 'get a ball' or 'get into groups of three' might be perfectly simple for adults, but can lead to chaos with twelve-year-olds. At least in the early stages of teaching, these organizational issues need to be

carefully planned. Therefore, lesson plans ought to include some guidance on grouping pupils for a coming task.

Monitoring and assessment

In order to determine whether the lesson has been effective in facilitating pupils' learning, it is vital that the teacher monitors and assesses their performance and progress. Rather than being merely responsive to feedback, it is necessary for the teacher 'to be active, and to probe, question, check whether the progress and attainment intended are occurring' (Kyriacou, 1991, p. 25). There are many opportunities to assess pupils in physical education lessons. Of course, the teacher can observe and note pupils' reactions as they move through the lesson. However, if used alone, observation can be of limited value. Pupils can be highly skilled at concealing difficulties (Pye, 1988), and further strategies are necessary to probe their understanding or performance. Transition phases can be used for questioning. Moreover, physical education incorporates numerous opportunities for pupils to demonstrate their understanding, although this needs to be planned in a sensitive way to avoid placing an individual under undue pressure.

One example of a lesson plan is offered in Figure 3.5. (Alternative models can be found in Bailey, 2001a, PEA, 1995, and Read and Edwards, 1992.)

Creating context

Bott (1997, p. 30) describes the skill development phase as the most important part of the lesson, and Gallahue (1993, p. 198) states that 'only after the skill has been reasonably mastered should it be incorporated into game-like activities'. However, this is ignoring the great amount of skill development that occurs implicitly as a result of a well-chosen game or activity. This is especially the case for younger pupils and those with learning difficulties, where pupils sometimes have difficulty identifying the context or meaning of a particular skill. For this reason, there may be times when the 'skill development' part of a lesson needs to be placed in context. For example, it would be ridiculous to work on the details of a competent swimmer's strokes before creating the context of that detail (by letting the child swim). In games, also, specific skills only make sense in relation to the game of which they are a part. Pupils need to understand the game as a whole in order to appreciate how the different skill elements fit together. In this approach, the teacher's role is one of facilitation and intervention, offering help with specific

Lesson Plan			
Theme: Learning objectives:		Date/time: Class/no. of pupils:	
Reference to statutory requirements:			
Resources & lesson preparation:			
Phase/timing	Pupils' activities	Teaching & safety points	Assessment
Introduction (Warm-up)			
Development			
Conclusion (Cool down)			

Figure 3.5   *An example lesson plan template*

problems or extending a child's repertoires of skills. For this reason, an alternative model of planning some activities may be more appropriate:

1) warm-up
2) game activity
3) skill development
4) game activity
5) conclusion
(see Chapter 2 for more details).

Non-participants

Physical education places particular demands upon pupils, and it sometimes happens that individuals are unable to participate because of injury or ill-health. This ought to be a rare occurrence: if pupils are well enough to be in school, they are usually well enough to take part in physical education lessons. But, of course, there are exceptions, such as broken bones, and the teacher needs to offer worthwhile alternative activities for these non-participants. Sitting in the corner of the gym reading or doing mathematics is not a valid option! Instead, the teacher should plan activities in which pupils can engage and which relate to the main theme of the lesson, but do not involve active physical participation. These alternative roles can include: coaching others, umpiring, taking the role of commentator or sports journalist, choreographing dances or recording performances using information and communication technologies.

Conclusion

This chapter has suggested that planning is an essential feature of effective teaching in physical education. The planning needs of teachers vary from individual to individual. Some physical educators plan in great detail, whilst others produce plans that are relatively brief. Whatever the style, teachers should be fully prepared, but should not feel that they are a slave to their plans. Teachers should be willing to divert from the lesson plan to follow an exciting new development or issue that crops up whilst teaching, in the secure knowledge that a well-planned lesson acts as a safety net to which they can return when required. This allows effective planning to support their own and the pupils' development and achievement in physical education.

CHAPTER 4

The Effective Use of Teaching Styles

Introduction

The use of appropriate teaching styles makes an important contribution to pupils' learning in physical education and is not something that can be left to chance. Teaching styles are concerned with *how* an activity is delivered, rather than *what* is delivered. For Siedentop (1991) a teaching style is typified by the instructional and managerial climate that exists during the lesson, and is most clearly observed in the teacher's interactions with pupils. He goes on to identify a teacher's instructional format as 'the different ways teachers organise the delivery of instruction, and particularly, how the student role changes as a result of the changing format' (p. 228).

In England and Wales, the National Curriculum for Physical Education (DfEE/QCA, 1999) instructs teachers what to teach (content) but not how to do it, leaving them the scope and responsibility to choose different instructional methods. Different teaching styles affect many important aspects of the teaching process, including the lesson's 'climate', time-on-task, pupil input and the teacher's ability to meet individual needs. As Kizer and colleagues (1984, p. 91) have pointed out, 'although knowledge of subject matter is absolutely necessary, good teaching technique will greatly enhance the effectiveness of the teacher'.

This chapter focuses on the spectrum of teaching styles proposed by Mosston and Ashworth (1986). After consideration of the research evidence and current teacher utilization of the different styles, the debate centres on the advantages and disadvantages of the direct, teacher-centred styles compared to their indirect, pupil-centred alternatives. It outlines some general guidance when teaching with each approach. The chapter then reflects on why a variety of teaching styles is important in secondary physical education and what other factors may influence a teacher's choice of instructional method.

The Spectrum of Teaching Styles

In their highly influential text, Mosston and Ashworth (1986) propose a spectrum of teaching styles, which they see not as techniques or approaches but as 'a framework of options in the relationships between teacher and learner' (Mosston, 1992, p. 56). The spectrum incorporates ten landmark styles along a continuum (see Figure 4.1), and is based around the central importance of *decision making* in the teaching process, which governs all of the behaviours that follow. These include such fundamentals as how pupils are organized, and how the topic is presented. Decisions are grouped into pre-impact, impact and post-impact categories and include all the conceivable options that need to be made during the teacher–pupil interactions. The spectrum represents two key themes within the continuum: a direct, teacher-led approach, juxtaposed with an open-ended, pupil-centred style where the teacher acts as facilitator (see Table 4.1). As Mosston (1992, p. 29) notes: 'The spectrum defines the available options or styles, their decision structures, the specific roles of the teacher and the learner . . . and the objectives best reached by each style.'

The comprehensive nature of the spectrum permits a clear view of two central human capacities utilized in physical education:

- The capacity for *production* (of new knowledge, movements).
- The capacity for *reproduction* (of existing knowledge; e.g., replication of movements or techniques).

This is one of the key aspects relating to the use of teaching styles: *matching the appropriate style to the intended learning outcome(s) of the lesson*. Each style has its own strengths and weaknesses that can render it more or less useful in supporting pupil learning. As Mosston (1992. p. 28) has argued:

The fundamental issue in teaching is not which style is better or best, but rather which style is appropriate for reaching the

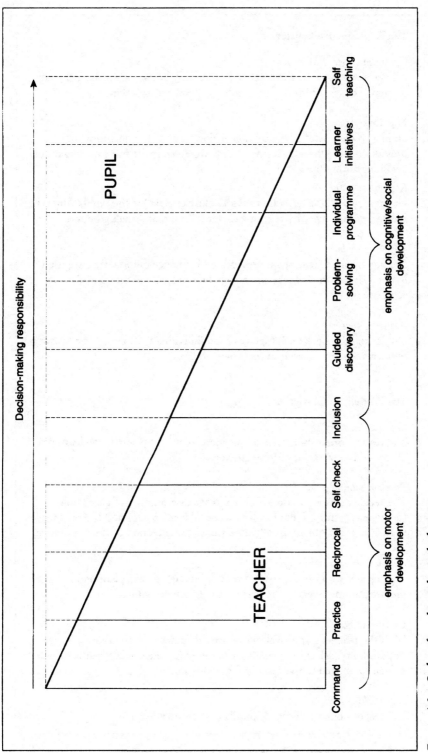

Figure 4.1 *Styles of teaching physical education*

The Reproductive Cluster

Command style
All decisions made by the teacher who usually breaks down the skill, step by step. The class respond uniformly to specific instructions.

Practice style
Similar to command as the teacher makes most of the decisions and provides the feedback to learners. The pupil can make some organizational decisions during the lesson.

Reciprocal style
Planned by the teacher, who provides clear criteria for the pupils who take greater responsibility by teaching each other in pairs/small groups.

Self-check style
Planned by the teacher who provides performance criteria, that are used by the learners to facilitate and assess their progress of motor skill acquisition.

Inclusion style
Similar to self-check but emphasis is on individuals, who start the task at a performance level geared to their own ability.

The Productive Cluster

Guided discovery style
The teacher presents a series of questions that lead (funnel) the learner to 'discover' (converge upon) the answer.

Problem-solving style
The teacher sets a question/problem that has a number of acceptable (divergent) solutions. Pupils often work in small groups and their response to solving the problem usually determines the direction of the next move.

Individual programme style
The teacher suggests the subject matter but the learner plans and designs the programme, seeking the teacher's help when required.

Learner-initiated style
With the teacher's approval, the learner assumes virtually full responsibility, selecting, planning and designing the subject matter which is then submitted to the teacher for evaluation.

Self-teaching style
Full responsibility is taken by pupils in their own learning.

Table 4.1 *Summary of the styles within Mosston's spectrum*

objectives of a given episode. Every style has a place in the multiple realities of teaching and learning.

Thus, only in exceptional circumstances (such as where safety is paramount) would one style be adopted for the whole lesson. Furthermore, the two capacities mentioned are very much complementary rather than mutually exclusive.

The Effectiveness of Different Teaching Styles

Despite a growing interest in teaching styles, research in this area is still generally equivocal, perhaps because of difficulty in measurement (Rink, 1993). However, there is strong empirical support for the effectiveness of direct instruction in certain contexts (Housner, 1990; Kizer et al., 1984). Within physical education, Mawer (1999 p. 98) recently claimed that 'there is certainly a growing body of evidence to suggest that direct teaching approaches ... may be effective for the learning of motor skills'. This may well be due to the aim of direct teaching to keep pupils engaged in the learning experience for a maximum amount of time, and Brady (1998) has found some evidence that when a task is practised repetitively, skill acquisition is enhanced (supported Beckett 1990). Goldberger (1992), reporting on his comparative research of practice, reciprocal and inclusion styles, found that although all three styles improved motor skill learning, the practice style consistently produced the best results. In support, Silverman (1991) believes that when mastery of basic skills is the goal, direct instruction has the edge over indirect methods.

If creativity or independence (group or individual) are the goals, indirect teaching may be more effective. Both Cleland (1994) and Goldberger (1995) found divergent problem-solving to be effective at improving learners' thinking skills. Anderson (1999) has suggested that strategic learners (those taught through a process-orientated style) are more likely to persist at a task despite failures, challenge themselves to use new skills and use their mistakes to alter subsequent attempts. Research into the development of critical thinking skills in physical education is beginning to suggest that more pupil-centred styles are effective tools for this purpose too (Mawer, 1999). There is, also, a growing research base for the effectiveness of 'co-operative learning' in physical education (Grineski, 1996). Work in co-operative learning is prepared and presented by the teacher, but is learner-centred, with pupils working in small groups to achieve a goal. Tasks set encourage interdependence, yet individuals are held accountable for their actions. According to the research, this approach is most helpful in improving teamwork and social skills, although cognitive and psychomotor goals can also be achieved (Grineski, 1996).

Research into the effectiveness of direct and indirect teaching styles (particularly the Teaching Games For Understanding [TGFU] approach) on Games is more extensive. Indirect styles have been found to be effective at improving learners' decision-making skills and game playing ability (e.g. tactical awareness). Research also suggests indirect teaching methods can be as effective as direct methods in promoting skill learning (e.g. Allison and Thorpe, 1997). Furthermore, Sport Education (Siedentop, 1994), which is built on the principles of indirect teaching, is beginning to produce some very promising results in terms of pupil learning (Carlson, 1995; Grant, 1992). Mosston (1992) believes that there is enough evidence attesting to the value of each style in his teaching spectrum. The challenge is how to use each style properly.

The Use of Teaching Styles in Physical Education

There is much we do not know about the teaching styles being used by secondary physical educators. The research available, however, continues to demonstrate that teacher-centred styles remain the preferred choice for many teachers (Curtner-Smith and Hasty, 1997; Evans *et al.*, 1996b). One reason for this may be that direct methods have worked well for teachers in one aspect of their teaching in the past, and they therefore stick with a 'winning' formula. Another reason is concerned with safety and control. Pupil misbehaviour, in particular, is a concern for teachers (Pieron, 1998), and command-style tactics may be employed to keep a tight rein. Similarly, with reduced curriculum physical education time available (Harris, 1994), teachers may prioritize direct methods as they usually provide a quicker way to get across the basic knowledge. This problem has been exacerbated by some physical education departments using short, blocked units of work, trying to fit in too many activities (OfSTED, 2001).

An over-reliance on the direct teaching styles can be problematic. OfSTED (1995, p. 5) has highlighted that the limited range of teaching strategies utilized by some physical educators is a key issue. Indeed, Mawer (1999, p. 97) has suggested that 'there is a developing image of UK PE teachers, and particularly men, using a restricted range of teaching approaches'. This is unfortunate in the light of HMI's (1993) observation that the impact of a broad curriculum can be diminished by a lack of variety in teaching. Research may also help to explain why 'sometimes there is insufficient physical or intellectual demand on pupils', who are presented with too few opportunities to plan or evaluate their own work (OfSTED, 1995, p. 10), and why for a large proportion of pupils, the ability to plan and evaluate their own and others' work remains a persistent weakness (OfSTED, 2001).

Direct Teaching Styles

Teacher-centred methods have many advantages. New teachers may wish to establish their personalities and authority, and get the pupils 'on side' quickly. In dance, for example, where reports demonstrate boys' body management skills are often poor or under developed (OfSTED, 1995, p. 3) a male teacher who leads by example can break down pupils' perceived barriers to the activity, and enhance pupil engagement with the task. These styles also help keep the lesson 'tight', so teachers can concentrate on their strengths, and not be exposed by a lack of experience/expertise in an unfamiliar activity. More positively, direct styles help to maximize teacher input to all pupils, leaving less chance for misunderstanding.

Many pupils are adept at copying what they see, so teacher-centred lessons can be an effective way of improving physical performance where pupils reproduce the desirable response to a skill, especially where content has a hierarchical structure and is primarily basic-skill-orientated (Rink, 1993). Direct instruction of the 'basics' of an activity can help pupils participate relatively quickly, with less chance of establishing bad habits. Such teaching can provide a foundation of skills on which later (indirect) practice may be based.

Safety is always a priority in physical education lessons. A command-style approach helps teachers to keep lessons safe, since they have greater control over what goes on than they have in indirect approaches. Furthermore, some secondary pupils may have insufficient understanding of their own ability to know at what level to attempt a task, or others may not see the risk of danger in attempting the same task as their friend. The teacher's judgement (e.g. risk assessment) will be necessary to cover any misjudgements and help place pupils at the right levels. Moreover, a teacher-centred approach is often the most efficient way to conduct a whole-class warm-up, to convey a lot of essential information quickly, or to make a link between two items during the lesson. The structured learning environment of direct styles means teachers find the command style effective for controlling behaviour and supervising large classes whose unwieldy size can be awkward.

Some of the so-called direct teaching methods promote more than replication. In the *reciprocal style*, where pupils take over the implementation of instructions to teach each other, their communication, social and cognitive skills are improved as 'the act of playing the teacher role is an opportunity for the pupil to think through the task and how to approach it . . . with greater understanding which facilitates practical learning' (Williams, 1993, p. 30). Research by Goldberger (1995) also found reciprocal teaching helped learners become more skilled at analysing movements and detecting errors.

Some critics argue that direct styles are restraining rather than liberating, and restrict the ability to retain and transfer information (Brady, 1998). Direct approaches can frustrate pupils who have their own ways of working, and risk inhibiting cognitive development since they 'fail to recognise the importance of involving students in the decision making process' (Hellison and Templin, 1991, p. 133). Many models 'may have overemphasised the need for immediate success and become mindless and meaningless exercises for many students' (Rink, 1999, p. 161), because skills have been practised in isolation. This is probably because the variability of practice, so vital for the preparation of utilizing the skill in the complex environment of a game, is lost (see Chapter 2).

Direct styles, characterized by a skills-based approach, tend to focus on the content rather than on the child. This can mean that 'less able pupils may never progress to understanding rules and tactics, making decisions and solving problems because they have not developed the skills to enable them to participate in the game' (Capel, 2000b, p. 91). Although pupils may be active for a lot of time, some critics question how *purposeful* this physical 'education' is, since the explanation given and the task set are likely to be inappropriate for many pupils.

One task set for the whole class is only likely to be appropriate for some pupils, too easy for others, and too difficult for the rest. Although able pupils will probably improve over the lesson, it may be that the task set actually restricts their performance (OfSTED, 2001). Less able pupils, too, can suffer, as activities often lack the flexibility to suit individual needs, which will clearly hamper learning. The dangerous 'knock-on' effect of a pupil working at the wrong level, is likely to be a loss of interest and hence concentration (OfSTED, 1995). The teacher must consider the need for pupil grouping in support of direct teaching, otherwise whole-class activities can result in 'individual needs not being adequately met' (HMI,1993, p. 7).

Teaching by direct methods can involve individualized tasks as the teacher can increase the freedom given to pupils through instruction: 'find a balance that uses one hand and one foot' (little freedom); 'balance on two body parts only' (increasing freedom), 'hold any balance for the count of five' (most freedom). As OfSTED (1995, p. 7) have pointed out, 'high standards are achieved where the skill element of an activity is appropriately matched to pupils' level of experience and ability'. Table 4.2 presents a summary of the key characteristics of direct teaching methods.

Indirect Teaching Styles

Weaknesses are clearly evident in direct teaching styles when learning outcomes are aimed at the creation of new ideas and movements, pupil analysis of performance, and personal and social development. In some instances, these approaches permit pupils little opportunity to plan and evaluate performance. If these aims are the teacher's focus, pupil-centred styles provide a valuable alternative.

It has often been proposed that pupils understand best if they are cognitively involved in the learning of a skill (Anderson, 1999), and that learning to learn through experimentation and problem-solving are critical features of a child's education. As Keighley (1993, p. 20) points out, 'physical activity does not guarantee mental activity and it is mental activity which produces learning'. Reports that secondary-aged pupils show limited tactical awareness (OfSTED, 1995) supports the case for more indirect teaching strategies that empower pupils to think for themselves to solve problems.

Indirect styles support pupils' investigation and problem-solving skills which may be particularly important in 'creative' situations, such as composing a dance or developing tactical 'know-how'. Indirect methods tend to ask higher order questions that require open-ended, intellectually challenging responses. It is argued that execution of the skill is enhanced through exploration that provides a richness and wholeness to the learning experience (Keighley, 1993).

Research suggests that pupils enjoy indirect styles (Kinchin *et al.*, 2001) as the activity can flow more without teacher interruptions and they are not required to go through repetitive and redundant drills (Mawer, 1999). The pupils in the class can be an excellent resource for managing the environment, generating ideas, collaborating with and motivating peers. By handing over some control to the

Direct teaching	Indirect teaching
Goals are usually explicit	*Goals* are usually more holistic and implicit
Product-orientated: suitable for learning most psychomotor discreet, closed skills (e.g., volleyball serve)	*Process-orientated*: suitable for serial, open skills (e.g., finding space in invasion games)
Consumption: pupils get to know information	*Construction*: pupils get to know how to use information
Formal: deliberate and calculated, so safety well controlled as teacher is central	*Informal*: open and flexible; teacher on periphery
Pupil dependence, producing *'Followership'*	Pupil independence, encouraging *Leadership*
Imitation: suits pupils who learn best by observing	*Innovation*: suits pupils who learn best by experimenting
Duplication: so less cognitively challenging	*Creation*: so more cognitively challenging
Can support pupils' affective development, but not primary concern	Strong development of pupil's *affective domain*
Limited differentiation	*Excellent differentiation*
Teacher is main resource	Greater use of *material resources*
Teacher as *coach*; *leader*	Teacher as *mentor*, *'enabler'*, co-investigator

Table 4.2   *Generalized features of direct and indirect teaching*

learners, indirect teaching methods empower pupils, and give them a sense of ownership of the lesson. This can have considerable effects on their motivation (Ames, 1992) an essential ingredient for learning (Biddle and Chatzisarantis, 1999).

Different teaching styles involve the pupil in learning in distinct ways and therefore have different potentials regarding motivation. Interesting research by Biddle (1999) suggests that pupils have greater intrinsic motivation to learn and more positive attitudes to physical education when the teacher creates a 'mastery' climate. Such a climate is characterized by the class being directed towards self-improvement and personal progress; effort is rewarded and choice is allowed, which are characteristics of pupil-centred methods. By contrast, a 'performance' climate leads to a much lower correlation with positive motivational outcomes. In support, research by Goudas and colleagues (1995) found teaching athletics in a 'differentiated' style (whose characteristics closely approximated those of 'indirect' styles) led to a high 'mastery' climate and more positive effects in terms of intrinsic motivation and task involvement than did lessons characterized by direct style teaching. A key reason for this could be that indirect methods embrace a number of solutions to a problem, rather than highlighting one best way; in this way they account for individual differences as everyone can experience success at some level.

Furthermore, research suggests pupils dislike normative comparisons with peers, that can be typical of some direct methods (such as command-and-practice styles). At its best, indirect work allows pupils time to think and reflect, to refine and to practise at the appropriate level so all pupils are able to achieve success at their particular level of ability. They may take longer to set up than direct teaching methods, but, once established, indirect styles facilitate purposeful participation.

Indirect styles not only commit pupils to 'having as go' at a task themselves but to greater social interaction. This has led Mawer (1995, p. 197) to conclude that,

> there appear to be considerable benefits in terms of both pupil learning gains and social development of teaching strategies that . . . involve peer teaching or peer support . . . provided the teaching programme is well structured and that pupils are trained for the role . . .

Some have claimed that pupil-centred approaches are too time-consuming: more time is spent thinking and discussing the activity than performing it (this point is debatable, however, as research on pupil-centred co-operative learning suggests that this method actually increases time on task [Grineski, 1996]). Motor skills are primarily learnt through practice rather than cognition, and Rink (1999) points out that the opportunity to learn a skill is the biggest single factor that predicts how much a child learns. Pupils who are not actually engaged in learning a motor task cannot learn it, so a significant characteristic of good instruction is provision for time-on-task (see Chapter 2). If open-ended styles are not carefully planned and controlled, lessons can easily 'drift', causing time to be wasted. Gallahue (1993) has suggested it is difficult to provide a framework of challenging movement tasks and to ensure continuity within and between lessons where teachers have not been trained appropriately for indirect teaching. If the work set is too broad, and virtually any pupil response will answer the question, standards of work can be low since pupils are insufficiently challenged (Williams, 1993).

During a lesson involving indirect methods, the teacher's role is more low key. However, a critical role is retained in creating significant learning opportunities, so lessons have to be carefully planned. Even where a lesson is dominated by an open-ended style, the teacher will always need to be at the ready. 'During the process of investigation and problem solving, effective teachers intervene to keep pupils on-track, to stimulate new avenues of enquiry, to break down tasks where necessary, and to maintain the momentum of the lesson' (OfSTED, 2001).

There are a number of issues that teachers need to be aware of when utilizing indirect methods. Clear success criteria are important alongside a framework for recording: the group should be given a limited number of clearly stated objectives to work to. As Rink (1993, p. 7) points out, '. . . merely engaging in an experience that has the potential to make a positive contribution to affective or cognitive goals does not ensure that these goals are met. Learning experiences must be designed and developed for specific outcomes . . .' (supported Freeman, 1998). Second, it cannot be assumed that because one or two central questions are posed the lesson will follow a natural, smooth course. It is invaluable for the teacher to circulate among pupils to check the agenda/task is being followed and use judicious questioning or suggestions to nudge the work to a higher level. Third, allowing pupils to work at their own pace still involves them meeting clear deadlines (based on OfSTED, 2001).

In the longer term, teachers should make sure pupils have been given sufficient guidance and practice in the 'basics' (the key generic movement principles behind running, jumping and throwing; see Macfadyen *et al.*, 2000) to allow them to work effectively (e.g. to provide worthwhile feedback to peers). It will also be useful for pupils to develop their research skills and the ability to analyse problems so they can identify how the basic skills are to be applied.

When a teacher starts to use indirect styles that the class are not used to, not too much should be expected of the pupils too soon. Indirect methods can bring fairly radical changes to the structure of the lesson so they need to be bedded in quite carefully. Pupils can be given independence gradually, through joint decision-making exercises at first. Using a couple of different teaching styles initially, will help prevent confusion and insecurity. Using a *problem-solving* approach to extend pupils' understanding of a topic previously taught didactically is one such example, and pupils can be afforded the opportunity to choose equipment (from a limited range), lead part of the warm-up, and demonstrate to the rest of the class. The inclusion style is also an excellent method to start with, as both the teacher and pupil are fully involved in the decision-making; the former decides content and presentation but the latter chooses the degree of difficulty at which to work. However, the teacher still needs to create an appropriate working environment first: 'for inclusion to work, students have to understand how to do it and have to feel comfortable choosing easier challenges' (Hellison and Templin, 1991, p. 61).

As pupils increase in competence and confidence in decision-making, they become ready to take more serious decisions. This can include planning the layout of the gymnasium, acting as coaches/ referees, and even planning a negotiated scheme of work. To complement these outcomes pupils must also develop the social skills to work productively.

Variety is the Spice of Life

Skilful physical education teaching is a difficult and complex job. Practitioners need to be able to cope with pupils' different personalities, experiences, developmental stages and learning abilities, as well as the very different nature of certain activities and the locations in which they must be taught. Only the utilization of a variety of approaches would seem to suffice if pupils are to receive the breadth and depth of teaching they need and deserve. Indeed, it may be that direct and indirect approaches work best in tandem (Gallahue, 1993); a repertoire of teaching styles can be a potent weapon in keeping the class interested and enthused. By mixing various styles the teacher can prevent an over-reliance on one style, and keep pupils from disengaging from their activity and learning.

Direct teaching methods are used first and foremost to ensure pupils gain a solid foundation in learning a new skill in a safe, controlled environment. Then, as pupils prove their competence and require more room to experiment and develop, the teacher can 'open up' the lesson, utilizing more indirect methods. Teacher-led sections of a lesson, such as the warm-up, can be an essential preparation for more independent group work that is to follow (OfSTED, 2001). Alternatively, the teacher may start with an open task that facilitates pupils working independently and 'having a go'. However, once they have reached a point where their inspiration has dried up, and frustration may ensue, the teacher can step in, as necessary, to direct pupils and help them reach the next level of understanding.

Different children have their own ways of learning, and there is no guarantee a pupil will initially 'connect' with a task presented in a certain way, so a repertoire of teaching styles is necessary. Moreover, research suggests that pupils who are exposed to a 'dynamic disequilibrium' caused by exposure to new and different forms of teaching and learning, will develop intellectually and move towards a more advanced level of information processing (Joyce and Weil, 1986).

Teaching Styles for Secondary School Physical Education

It would be unwise to make any attempt to prescribe specific ways of using different teaching styles given the very different nature of physical education classes. It is for the thoughtful practitioner to decide when and where the use of a certain style will be effective. However, it is hoped that some general guidance will be of assistance to those considering development of their teaching styles repertoire. It is to be noted that a teaching style is flexible only within the boundaries of what it is supposed to achieve (Mosston, 1992). As no one method covers all eventualities '. . . the effective teacher will have the ability to switch, mix, and blend teaching strategies to suit his objectives and pupil responses' (Mawer, 1995, p. 228). The National Curriculum for Physical Education (for England and Wales) (DfEE/QCA, 1999) provides an ideal example of the need for a variety of teaching styles due to the different demands placed on pupils (see Table 4.3).

If teachers are to implement these diverse directives it is clear that various teaching styles will be required. The Practice style, for

Acquire and develop skills

KS 3: *'refine* and *adapt* existing skills'

KS 4: *'develop* and apply advanced skills and techniques'

Select and apply skills, tactics and compositional ideas

KS 3: 'use principles to *plan* and *implement* strategies'

KS 4: *'apply* rules and conventions for different activities'

Evaluate and improve performance

KS 3: 'take the *initiative* to *analyse* their own and others' work'

KS 4: *'make informed choices* about what *role* they want to take in each activity'

Knowledge and understanding of fitness and health

KS 3: 'how to go about *getting involved* in activities that are good for their personal and social health and well being'

KS 4: 'how to *design* and *carry out* activity and training programmes'

(Taken from DfEE/QCA, 1999; *emphasis added*)

Table 4.3 *National Curriculum strands, showing the need for a variety of teaching styles*

example, can enhance pupils' ability to acquire skills, whereas the requirement for pupils to 'develop leadership skills' (DfEE/QCA, 1999, p. 23) may be better served by guided discovery methods or even the learner initiative style for older pupils.

Teachers must consider a number of basic factors when deciding which styles to use. The lesson must be safe, and the time, equipment and facilities available may influence what is possible. In a limited space the teacher may decide that closely directing pupils' movements is the only safe way to teach, or in a short lesson, the practice style might best maximize the limited time available. The characteristics of the pupils in a class are critical. Pupils with Special Educational Needs have been increasingly integrated into mainstream schools over recent years (see Chapter 7). Consequently, teachers now require an ever more flexible approach to cope with pupils' strengths and weaknesses, and teaching styles that can modify the learning environment will play an important role (Thompson, 1998). A pupil who has movement difficulties, for example, is likely to need greater time practising skills, and need more teacher guidance, which may be more suitable to direct teaching in the first instance.

In terms of teaching more able pupils, considerable research (e.g. Freeman, 1998; Van Tassel-Baska, 1994) highlights the educational value of allowing this group to work independently, to construct solutions to problems in a more unstructured environment, since they are particularly stimulated and challenged when actively involved in their own learning (HMI, 1993; see Chapter 8). It would also seem reasonable to suggest that motivated pupils will also do well using the productive styles since they 'invite' the learner to perform (Gallahue, 1993). The divergent style, for example, allows pupils to plan and follow their own devised pathways to reach a solution. Rink (1993) suggests non-conforming pupils perform better in structured environments characteristic of direct instruction. Less able pupils also seem to do better under command and practice conditions (Goldberger, 1992; Harrison *et al.*, 1995), perhaps because they need the more rigid framework and the greater reassurance/feedback provided by the teacher.

Some younger secondary pupils may have little understanding of certain areas of the curriculum, suggesting that initially the teacher will have to play a central role. Younger children often need very clear structures and boundaries, and constant reminders to ensure on-task activity. Therefore, the more formal methods of direct teaching may be helpful at certain points in the first year or two of secondary schooling. For example, teachers may need the command style to help keep over-enthusiastic pupils focused, especially where their relatively short attention spans require the teacher to intervene regularly to move children on to the next task.

The level of pupil comprehension is another factor to note. Some pupils will not be able to cope with the demands made on them by pupil-centred methods, which to work successfully, require children to have both developed verbal skills and a sound knowledge base from which to start. Older children will generally be more capable of benefiting from the pupil-centred approaches as their greater maturity and experience will complement the characteristics of indirect styles.

By secondary school many children will want to work with more freedom than at a younger age and will be less willing to accept uncritically routines and practices they believe to be childish. The teacher will need teaching styles that match pupils' views of their own development if teacher–pupil relationships are to remain positive. It seems inappropriate to 'command' a Year 12 pupil to do something, and although direct styles at times will benefit learning, the teacher may well get a better response by using indirect styles that give pupils more freedom and responsibility. The maturation of secondary-aged children's physical, cognitive and social skills can mean many of them successfully operating within the indirect teaching styles that lie towards the end of the continuum. OfSTED (1995, p. 11) report post-sixteen physical education is most successful when teachers 'provide activities that challenge students to apply their knowledge . . . Success is also achieved when students are enabled to work with an appropriate degree of independence.'

Pupils will also need to be prepared for the demands of GCSE and Advanced-level examination work, which require them to plan, perform and evaluate their work at a high level and to critically apply their knowledge. OfSTED (2001) reports that good Advanced level work generally involves problem-solving. Teachers will need to establish the right conditions for pupils to practise these skills and the teaching styles adopted will be a critical ingredient. Challenging pupils to research and present a topic to their peers often works well in examination classes.

Conclusion

How you teach is just as important as *what* you teach. It is vital for teachers to be able to use a variety of styles to meet pupils' differing needs. Only in this way can they ensure a safe, effective and positive learning environment. A 'one-size-fits-all' policy is wholly inappropriate to physical education and where teachers use direct styles they must ensure differentiation of tasks. If teachers are to celebrate the diversity of talent that exists in the secondary school, they need an equally diverse set of teaching methods to enable children to reach their own level of excellence.

Direct and indirect styles are not 'either–or' paradigms that teachers must slavishly decide between. Rather, they should be viewed as complementary methods providing the physical education teacher with a choice in how best to support pupils' learning. Perhaps the key question in choosing a teaching style should be 'Will it effectively get across the particular skills, knowledge or understanding I intend pupils to acquire or develop?'. Since both direct and indirect approaches have different strengths and weaknesses, utilizing a combination of the two seems the most sensible way forward.

CHAPTER 5

Assessing Learning and Achievement

Introduction

Assessment lies at the heart of effective teaching and learning in physical education. Since the advent of National Curricula in the United Kingdom, the role and importance of assessment procedures have been further stressed, and placed within a statutory framework. It is conceivable that a pupil can learn something worthwhile without assessment (after all, people can learn from pictures, television images or computers). But teaching is likely to be far more effective when lessons reflect the assessment of pupils' previous performances and experiences, and when their performances are observed, assessed and feedback is given by a knowledgeable person. As Piotrowski (2000, p. 51) pus it: 'Assessment is not necessarily integral to all teaching, but it is integral to good teaching.'

However, it is sometimes suggested that teachers of physical education remain unclear about what they should expect of pupils of different ages, and hence what they should be assessing. This view is given credence by inspection reports claiming that assessment is a relatively weak feature of physical education provision, needing development and support (Clay, 1997; OHMCI, 1998). This chapter discusses the purposes, forms and methods of assessment in physical education. In doing so, it seeks to offer the teacher guidance in the effective use of assessment.

What is Assessment?

Assessment in education is concerned with obtaining and interpreting information about pupils' skills, knowledge and understanding, and their learning needs. It usually involves two elements: description and judgement. The descriptive aspect of assessment is self-evident: in assessing a pupil or a group of pupils, the teacher aims to build up an accurate and fair portrait of their performance in a lesson or over a period of time. This information can inform future planning and teaching, and ultimately supports pupil learning. But as Carroll (1994) argues persuasively, assessment also involves the teacher making a *judgement*; the teacher does not simply note what pupils have done, but also makes some sort of qualitative statement about it. These judgements might involve comparisons with pupils' earlier performance, or with other pupils of the same age, or against some predetermined standards.

Informal assessment is common in all forms of teaching. Parents correct their children's errors, and make suggestions aimed at improving their performance of skills all of the time, just as teachers and sports coaches do. Corrections, feedback and support seem to be essential for some types of learning. There may be some skills and knowledge that would be simply impossible for the learner to obtain without the intervention of another, knowledgeable person (Bailey, 2001b). Informal assessment seems to be a natural process for humans, and inextricably linked to teaching and learning.

Formal assessment, on the other hand, has been traditionally associated with rather solemn experiences, like written tests or examinations. In the past, they were largely directed towards the so-called 'academic' subjects, like mathematics and history (Brown, 1994). 'Practical' subjects like physical education did not have formal assessment of this sort, and it is only in recent years that they have started to appear, such as in GCSE and Advanced level programmes (see Chapter 6). When physical education teachers did engage in formal sorts of assessment, they tended to focus on three forms:

- Comments on the school reports.
- National Governing Body award schemes.
- Selection of school teams.

These assessments were often based on limited evidence, lack of specific criteria, lack of systematic observation and recording and a reliance on general impressions (Carroll, 1994). Consequently, until the appearance of the National Curriculum, assessment in physical education was rarely seen as an important issue, and it did not receive the treatment given in many other subjects. As anybody familiar with schools and teaching today will know, that has all changed.

The last two decades or so have witnessed considerable changes to the policy and practice of assessment in all subjects. Assessment is now understood in a much broader way, and is recognized as a central and necessary ingredient of effective teaching and learning. Whilst there is debate regarding the details of its implementation, there is consensus among writers on physical education that the subject needs to align itself to these trends (cf. Piotrowski, 2000; Carroll, 1994; Spackman, 1998).

The most significant trend in recent assessment practice relates to the way in which it has progressed from traditional notions of testing for selection to much broader aims (Brown, 1994). As discussed, physical education's emphasis on assessment for the identification of school teams paralleled wider practices in which examinations were used primarily for selection of young people for further study or careers. Its purpose was often more to do with public relations for the school than the needs of the pupils. Assessment is now seen as fulfilling a range of purposes, including fostering of pupil learning, improving teaching, recording achievement and informing learners of available options. This change has been associated with a move away from reliance upon assessment *at the end* of a programme, to a recognition that assessment can inform and improve performance *throughout* the programme.

There has also been an increase in the range of aspects assessed. Examinations assess a narrow range of knowledge and understanding. They are less suited to measuring pupils' social skills and attitudes, nor are they very useful for assessing the *application* of skills and knowledge. Following on from the earlier point, if assessment is going to inform teaching and learning during a programme, it needs to acknowledge the full scope of factors impacting upon that teaching and learning. Physical education, in particular, involves the performance of skills and the application of knowledge and understanding in specific contexts, and this highlights the need for assessment procedures that are flexible enough to acknowledge this.

A third trend has been to devolve responsibility for assessment (Brown, 1994). Teachers have always carried out assessment, often on the behalf of external agencies like examination boards or governing bodies for sports. The fuller recognition of assessment's relationship to learning has led to much more diverse practice, with pupils being expected to take greater responsibility for the learning and assessment of themselves and their peers. With an increase in vocational training and work experience within the mainstream curriculum, there has been an expectation that employers, too, become involved in the assessment process.

Purposes of Assessment

In light of the previous discussion, it is possible to set out some fundamental purposes of assessment in physical education.

The primary role of assessment relates to the *improvement of learning and teaching*. Assessment can give feedback to pupils, allowing them to evaluate and improve their own performance. It can also provide valuable information about pupils' progress, and this allows teachers to evaluate the effectiveness of their teaching by assessing how well the learning objectives have been achieved. Assessment is also a factor in encouraging pupils to strive to succeed and improve their skills, knowledge and understanding, and, as such, can act as a source of motivation for pupils.

Assessment can be the means for *communicating the nature and level of pupils' achievement* at specific points in their schooling. This information can be used for a number of purposes, including the traditional ones of selection and certification, which still play an important role for both society and the individual. Qualifications indicate a satisfactory level of ability that should enable an individual to carry out work in a safe and competent manner. So, for example, we will generally feel more comfortable putting our trust in a climbing instructor who has demonstrated a recognized standard of attainment in relevant skills, than someone who has failed to do so.

Finally, assessment can be used for *diagnostic purposes*. It can help identify a pupil's strengths and weaknesses, difficulties and needs, in order to inform planning and teaching. Diagnostic assessments are frequently used to detect special needs in a particular area. Physical education teachers have a range of strategies available to them to assist in the identification of movement problems (cf. Bailey and Robertson, 2000; Sugden, 1991; Henderson and Sugden, 1992). There are also more generic approaches, such as those associated with the *Code of Practice on the Identification and Assessment of Special Educational Needs* (DFE, 1994) that can be utilized.

There are, of course, numerous other purposes of assessment, including the following:

- To assist planning for differentiation (see Chapter 7).
- To compare pupils (with others in a class, year, school, or nationally).
- To inform judgements regarding accountability (to help judge the effectiveness of the school).
- To select for future education or training (e.g., levels of entry requirements for university).
- To discriminate between pupils (e.g., streaming by ability, or examination grades).
- To select for specific purposes (e.g., school teams).

Issues of Assessment in Physical Education

The practical nature of much of the physical education curriculum presents certain difficulties with regard to assessing learning or performance. Piotrowski (2000, p. 50) summarizes the problem:

> Teachers are largely judging practical performances, which, by their nature, are transitory. The actions are often fleeting and there is usually no permanent record in the form of written, painted or crafted objects for the teacher to view and return to in formulating a judgement. In this context, there remains a danger of physical education assessments being inaccurate, unreliable, subjective or simply too vague to offer worthwhile information.

So, in order to make fair and accurate assessments of pupils' learning or performance in physical education, the teacher needs to adhere to certain principles of good practice. These principles, which are of central importance if measurement is to be worthwhile, are summarized below (cf. Carroll, 1994, and Bailey, 2001a):

- validity
- reliability
- objectivity
- practicality.

Validity refers to whether the assessment protocol actually assesses what is supposed to be assessed. Valid assessment accurately represents pupils' attainment in a *specific context*. This has important implications for physical education, since it implies that the most valid forms of assessment are those that are as close as possible to the actual skills, knowledge and understanding being assessed. Practical performance cannot be sensibly measured through paper-and-pencil tests, for example, since they assess different competencies.

So, the teacher needs to look for more meaningful and specific approaches.

One way of proceeding is by ensuring *content validity* (Gipps and Stobart, 1993). This refers to matching the assessment task as closely as possible to the *objectives* of a particular lesson or unit of work. At the least, this approach offers coherence between teachers' planning, teaching and assessment, but it also has the potential to make assessment more focused and useful. The lesson objectives indicate the skills, knowledge and understanding that are expected to be reached by the end of a specific period of time (such as the end of a lesson, or a unit of work). A difficulty is that a great deal of learning in physical education, such as understanding, attitudes, feelings and values, is somewhat 'invisible', and not accessible to simple measurement. How can we record what is going on in the head of a learner? Fortunately, learning of this sort may be reflected in certain types of explicit *behaviours*, and these are observable and assessable. For example, whether a pupil understands the use of extension and articulation of movement in gymnastics might be assessed by observing that pupil performing in a carefully planned activity (perhaps by performing a sequence requiring a number of extended and articulated actions). This can then be followed up with focused questioning ('Why did you hold your legs in that way during the routine?').

Reliability in assessment is defined as ensuring consistency and comparability of practices. Whilst validity relates to the accuracy of assessment, reliability refers to its fairness: 'in the circumstances, would the teacher give the same assessment on another occasion, or would other teachers give the same assessment?' (Carroll, 1994, p. 16). Making a reliable judgement of attainment involves an awareness of the different factors that can influence performance, such as the context of the assessment, the standards applied to the assessment and sheer chance. Reliability in assessment has taken on an increased significance with the advent of examinations in physical education, in which teachers' judgements need to be comparable not only with colleagues in their own school, but nationally or even internationally (see Chapter 6).

There are numerous strategies that teachers have employed to improve the reliability of their assessment in physical education, including:

• Devising shared understandings of Standards (e.g., what would it really look like if a pupil could 'analyse and comment on

their own and others' work, . . . showing that they understand how skills (and) tactics . . . relate to the quality of the perform- ance'? (National Curriculum for Physical Education, 1999, p. 43).
- Team teaching and shared assessment of a specific group.
- Observing video-recorded performances, and discussing levels of attainment witnessed.
- Devising agreed, explicit criteria for the identification of tal- ented pupils.
- Inviting external colleagues for moderation purposes.
  (See also SCAA, 1995, for more generic, non-PE strategies.)

Closely related to the need for reliability is the principle of objectiv- ity, which refers to the extent to which assessment does not reflect personal or institutional bias. Of course, a great deal of physical education work does not lend itself to objective measurement, and will necessarily be based on somewhat subjective interpretations and judgements on the part of the teacher (Carroll, 1994). Nonetheless, it may be that some judgements merely express personal prejudice in terms of, perhaps, gender, ethnicity or social background. Morti- more and colleagues (1994) carried out a review of the literature on teacher expectations related to different groups within schools, and some of their findings are of relevance to the present discussion. For example, they found that pupils from non-manual family back- grounds are rated as of higher ability than pupils from manual backgrounds. Boys generally receive a greater amount of criticism than girls, from both male and female teachers. However, teachers also tend to rate boys slightly more favourably than girls in terms of ability, even after account has been taken of attainment. These unwarranted judgements do not seem to be the result of a premedi- tated decision by teachers to favour one group over another, and presumably reflect wider societal expectations. As professionals, physical education teachers need to be aware of these expectations, and strive not to allow them to distort their assessments of pupils' performance, or their more general dealings with pupils.

There is a risk of over-compensating for the difficulties associated with assessment in physical education, by drawing up schemes that are time-consuming, or which take the teacher away from proper supervision of the lesson. Therefore, as Bailey (2001a, p. 143) sug- gests 'the challenge for teachers of physical education is to find a system of assessment that fulfils the principles of good practice without preventing them from carrying out their other duties'.

Effective assessment in physical education requires the teacher to strike a balance between the demand for detail and the necessity for practicality. Schemes that provide a great deal of information on pupils, but which are massively time-consuming, will either interfere with a teacher's primary responsibility, to teach, or will not be done. Schemes that are easy to use, but which do not provide sufficient detail for planning, teaching or reporting purposes, are worthless.

Methods of Assessment in Physical Education

Traditionally, physical educators have drawn on a rather narrow range of evidence in support of their assessment of pupils' learning and attainment. Physical fitness tests, athletics records and drills may contribute information, but are, in themselves, inadequate. As has been discussed above, recent developments in assessment practice have stressed the importance of teachers building up a fuller picture of pupils' abilities and understandings, and not all of these are readily observable. Therefore, a variety of assessment strategies is essential. One way of appreciating this variety is by considering the assessment decisions that teachers need to make.

Formal or informal assessment?

One way of distinguishing assessment approaches relates to the context in which it takes place. The great majority of assessment activity is rather informal, and occurs as part of normal physical education teaching. Teachers observe, provide feedback and make mental notes regarding pupils' performance and understanding. At special times, though, assessment fulfils more formal functions, such as examinations, qualifications and selection.

Internal or external assessment?

This distinction refers to the control of assessment. Internal assessment is devised and carried out by the teacher or pupils as part of the everyday teaching programme. External assessment, in contrast, is devised by external agencies (such as examination boards, central government, national governing bodies for sport), and is usually associated with qualifications or awards.

Formative or summative assessment?

These terms refer to the purposes and use of assessment. Formative assessment is on-going, and takes place during the teaching and learning process. It involves describing pupils' progress, offering feedback and identifying their future needs. As such, formative assessment is fundamentally concerned with the improvement of future learning. Summative assessment takes place at the end of a specified period of time (such as a unit of work, Key Stage or a course). It is essentially concerned with the measurement or identification of attainment or performance.

Criteria-referenced, Norm-referenced or Ipsative-referenced Assessment?

This distinction refers to the standard against which a judgement is made. Criteria-referenced assessment involves making comparisons of what pupils know, understand or can do in relation to predetermined criteria or standards. National Curriculum level descriptions and national governing body awards both provide examples of this form of assessment, since pupils are judged with regard to whether or not their performance or understanding fulfils existing criteria. Norm-referenced assessment is a comparison of an individual's or group's performance with that of others. An example of norm-referenced assessment would be when pupils are tested during an athletics or swimming lesson, their times are recorded, and based upon this information, pupils are divided into ability groups for differentiated teaching. Ipsative assessment, by contrast, involves a comparison of pupils' current achievement with their previous performances in the same activity. This approach is often most useful when used in formative assessment situations and for motivating pupils, by highlighting their improvement and development. Carroll (1994) has stressed that criteria-, norm- and ipsative-referenced forms of assessment need not be mutually exclusive, and can be profitably used together in support of pupils' learning. So, criteria for specific tasks can be based on normative expectations of pupils' work, and ipsative assessment can help pupils set the criteria for their future performances.

Validity, reliability, objectivity and practicality set the boundaries within which assessment should be operated, but they still allow a range of approaches. Informal forms of assessment, such as on-going observation and questioning, occur throughout the pupils' physical education experience. More formal measures, such as end-of-unit assessments and examinations take place at specific times. In all cases, though, it is important that the teacher is very clear about what is to be assessed, and the most appropriate way of doing so.

It need not be only the teacher who gathers information. The pupils themselves can significantly contribute to the assessment. The side-effect of involving pupils in their own assessment is that the process can greatly develop their understanding of the task being assessed. 'Pupils can be actively involved in their own assessment: reviewing their work and progress; setting future targets for learning; and deciding, in discussion with the teacher, which pieces of work provide evidence of particular attainments' (SEAC, 1992). Pupils can engage in assessment of their own performance and that of their peers.

Some commentators (e.g., Piotrowski, 2000; Wetton, 1988) have complained physical educators have been given insufficient guidance with regard to the levels of performance and understanding that are appropriate to expect from pupils of particular age ranges. In response to such accusations, many countries have established frameworks that attempt to translate the broader educational aims of the subject (see Chapter 1) into progressive expectations for pupils of different ages and experiences. The National Curriculum for Physical Education in England and Wales (DfEE/QCA, 1999) is an example of such a scheme (see Table 5.1).

Recording

Every teacher needs to maintain records of pupils' attainment and communicate this attainment with relevant groups. Whilst these processes are often considered tedious and time-consuming, recording and reporting are important features of pupil assessment. Recording of pupil attainment, in particular, represents a large part of the mounting paperwork about which many teachers justifiably complain. However, as will be suggested here, there is no need to compile elaborate documentation, and the most effective recording and reporting procedures are those that are simple and manageable.

Record-keeping fulfils a number of functions for the physical education teacher. These include:

- Recording pupils' progress and attainment.
- Supporting continuity of experiences throughout schooling.
- Communicating information to other teachers.
- Giving feedback to pupils and parents.
- Helping to identify problems, gaps in experience and specific needs.
- Informing reporting to parents, school managers and external agencies.
- Informing planning and differentiation.

In light of the earlier discussion on methods, record-keeping relates to both formative and summative forms of assessment. Perhaps the central role for trainee and newly qualified teachers is one of informing future practice: 'what has worked, what has not?'; 'what range of abilities and needs are there in this class?'; 'how successful have my teaching strategies and materials proved in supporting learning and attainment?' As well as this formative function, teachers are also often required to draw conclusions about pupils' attainment, to make some sort of summative judgement about the level of skills, knowledge and understanding that have been reached by individuals or groups.

Traditionally, many schools have relied upon sporting national governing body awards as the basis for their record-keeping in physical education. These schemes can usefully supplement certain aspects of the curriculum, but their primary role is not the same as educational assessment. As such, they are inadequate as a foundation for an effective record-keeping system. This is because records need to focus on the learning and attainment of pupils during planned units and lessons.

The main point here is the same as in the earlier discussion of assessment in general: effective record-keeping strikes a balance between the demand for detail and the necessity for practicality. Table 5.2 offers an example of a record-keeping system that attempts to strike such a balance (from Bailey, 2001a; cf. Carroll, 1994; Headington, 2000). The recording sheet is completed by the teacher at the end of a unit of work. In this case, reference is made to pupil attainment in four themes within the National Curriculum for Physical Education (DfEE/QCA, 1999). There is also an opportunity for the teacher to make some qualitative, personal statements about pupils' work, interests or needs.

SEAC (1992) makes the following points about recording pupils' progress. Records should:

- Be simple to complete so that they do not cause too much interference in class activities and practices.
- Include all the relevant information so that they may readily inform decisions about future action.
- Be meaningful to others who may have access to them.
- Be accessible to pupils so that they can enhance pupils' understanding of the teaching, learning and assessment process.

Reporting

Teachers also need to communicate their assessment findings to other interested groups. In particular, there is a statutory requirement in

Level	Acquiring and developing skills	Selecting and applying skills	Evaluating and improving skills	Developing knowledge and understanding of fitness and health
1	Pupils copy, repeat and explore simple skills and actions with basic control and co-ordination.	They start to link these skills and actions in ways that suit the activities.	They describe and comment on their own and others' actions.	They talk about how to exercise safely, and how their bodies feel during an activity.
2	Pupils explore simple skills. They copy, remember, repeat and explore simple actions with control and co-ordination.	They vary skills, actions and ideas, and link these in ways that suit the activities. They begin to show some understanding of simple tactics and basic compositional ideas.	They talk about differences between their own and others' performance and suggest improvements.	They understand how to exercise safely, and describe how their bodies feel during different activities.
3	Pupils select and use skills, actions and ideas appropriately, applying them with co-ordination and control.	They show that they understand tactics and composition by starting to vary how they respond.	They can see how their work is similar to and different from others' work, and use this understanding to improve their own performance.	They give reasons why warming up before an activity is important, and why physical activity is good for their health.
4	Pupils link skills, techniques and ideas, and apply them accurately and appropriately.	Their performance shows precision, control and fluency, and that they understand tactics and composition.	They compare and comment on skills, techniques and ideas used in their own and others' work, and use this understanding to improve their performance.	They explain and apply basic safety principles in preparing for exercise. They describe what effects exercise has on their bodies, and how it is valuable to their fitness and health.
5	Pupils select and combine their skills, techniques and ideas and apply them accurately and appropriately, consistently showing precision, control and fluency.	When performing, they draw on what they know about strategy, tactics and composition.	They analyse and comment on skills and techniques and how these are applied in their own and others' work. They modify and refine skills and techniques to improve their performance.	They explain how the body reacts during different types of exercise, and warm up and cool down in ways that suit the activity. They explain why regular, safe exercise is good for their fitness and health.
6	Pupils select and combine skills, techniques and ideas.	They apply them in ways that suit the activity, with consistent precision, control and fluency. When planning their own and others' work, and carrying out their own work, they draw on what they know about strategy, tactics and composition in	They analyse and comment on how skills, techniques and ideas have been used in their own and others' work, and on compositional and other aspects of performance, and suggest ways to improve.	They explain how to prepare for, and recover from, the activities. They explain how different types of exercise contribute to their fitness and health, and describe how they might get involved in other types of activities and exercise.

7	Pupils select and combine advanced skills, techniques and ideas, adapting them accurately and appropriately to the demands of the activities. They consistently show precision, control, fluency and originality.	response to changing circumstances, and what they know about their own and others' strengths and weaknesses. Drawing on what they know of the principles of advanced tactics and compositional ideas, they apply these in their own and others' work. They modify them in response to changing circumstances and other performers.	They analyse and comment on their own and others' work as individuals and team members, showing that they understand how skills, tactics or composition and fitness relate to the quality of the performance. They plan ways to improve their own and others' performance. They explain the principles of practice and training, and apply them effectively.	They explain the benefits of regular, planned activity on health and fitness, and plan their own appropriate exercise and activity programme.
8	Pupils consistently distinguish and apply advanced skills, techniques and ideas, consistently showing high standards of precision, control, fluency and originality.	Drawing on what they know of the principles of advanced tactics or composition, they apply these principles with proficiency and flair in their own and others' work. They adapt them appropriately in response to changing circumstances and other performers.	They evaluate their own and others' work, showing that they understand the impact of skills, strategy and tactics or composition, and fitness on the quality and effectiveness of performance. They plan ways in which their own and others' performance could be improved. They create action plans and ways of monitoring improvement.	They use their knowledge of health and fitness to plan and evaluate their own and others' exercise and activity programme.
Exceptional Performance	Pupils consistently use advanced skills, techniques and ideas with precision and fluency.	Drawing on what they know of the principles of advanced strategies and tactics or composition, they consistently apply these principles with originality, proficiency and flair in their own and others' work.	They evaluate their own and others' work, showing that they understand how skills, strategy and tactics or composition, and fitness relate to and affect the quality and originality of performance. They reach judgements independently about how their own and others' performance could be improved, prioritizing aspects for further development.	They consistently apply appropriate knowledge and understanding of health and fitness in all aspects of their work.

Table 5.1   *The attainment targets for physical education*

KS/YEAR: UNIT:	Learning objectives of unit: 1. 2. 3. 4.				
Pupils' names	Acquiring and developing skills	Selecting and applying skills	Evaluating and improving skills	Knowledge and understanding of fitness and health	Comments

Table 5.2   *A record-keeping sheet*

England and Wales to make some report of pupils' achievement in physical education to parents every year. Reports are usually rather formal, internal processes of assessment, which can be formative, offering guidance and suggestions to support further learning, or summative, summarizing pupils' attainment at a given point of time. They can also be criteria-referenced, norm-referenced or ipsative-referenced: the report can make judgements based on pupils' attainment against existing level descriptions contained within a statutory framework (like the National Curriculum). Alternatively, the report can compare one pupil's attainment against the rest of a class, or against some expected standard for pupils of a specific age (although comparisons of pupils within a class is now rare in reports); or it can note progression and improvement of attainment from the last report.

The simplest and most effective reports are based on pupils' records throughout the year. In other words, the information that has been collected as part of the normal record-keeping carried out during teaching can be translated into a narrative about a pupil's attainment. This supports Clay's (1997) advice that reports should focus on achievement and skill development, rather than merely detailing activities covered and attitudes adopted. The emphasis in both recording and reporting should always be on the *learning* that has taken place.

Conclusion

This chapter has discussed a range of issues in planning and carrying out assessment in the specific context of physical education. It has been argued that assessment is closely related to pupil learning and achievement, and, therefore, is one of the corner stones of good practice. The underlying principles of assessment are neatly summarized by Harlen and her colleagues (1994, p. 275): 'The choice of different assessment procedures must be decided on the basis of the purpose for which the assessment is being undertaken. This may well mean employing different techniques for different assessment purposes.'

CHAPTER 6

Examinations in Physical Education

Introduction

The United Kingdom has seen a massive expansion in examination courses over the last fifteen years (Hayes and Stidder, 1999; OfSTED, 1998). To a large extent, this has stemmed from the assessment-led reforms of the 1980s. A central tenet to this policy was the reorganization of examinations. In the mid-1980s the amalgamation of the Certificate of Secondary Education (CSE) and the General Certificate of Education (GCE) led to the formation of the General Certificate of Secondary Education (GCSE). This new format gave physical education the ideal opportunity to bolster its academic credibility by joining the other curriculum areas in having an equivalent examination course for secondary school leavers.

This chapter is divided into four main sections. Initially discussion centres on the arguments made against the formation of examinations in physical education. The chapter then goes on to deliberate arguments for examinations in the subject. In the third part, consideration is given to a number of issues surrounding examinations in physical education. Lastly, the chapter reflects on the implications of teaching examination courses for teachers of physical education.

Arguments Against Examinations in Physical Education

Although examinations in physical education have generally been regarded as a success, a number of arguments were put forward in the 1960s and 1970s against their formation. These arguments have been neatly summarized by Carroll (1994):

- The difficulty of assessing qualitative aspects of movement and games, and lack of objectivity, except in athletics and swimming.
- The most significant aspect of physical education could not be validly measured. (However, it was not stated what this aspect was.)
- The difficulty of comparing activities.
- Differences in individual development (e.g., physical).
- Difficulty of seeing the purpose or value: compromising physical education's own intrinsic motivation.

These arguments have come to be seen as unsubstantial and without evidence. Of course, a number of these objections can apply with equal force to other subjects, such as art and music. However, at the time they were influential in resisting developments in physical education. Moreover, to some extent they affected how the examination courses took shape.

Examinations meant that physical educators had to accept some form of outside influence and hence loss of freedom. Like all subjects, once physical education entered the realm of examinations it meant entry into the world of inter-school comparisons and the implicit pressure to select the best children to take the subject. Furthermore, it has been argued that the pressure of achieving successful examination results may necessitate a department to relegate other traditionally important aspects of their work (e.g., sport for all and extra-curricular clubs).

Dickenson and Almond (1987) remind us that GCSE and Advanced ('A') level examinations are not the only forms of accreditation, nor are they necessarily the most suitable medium to gather evidence of pupils' achievements and experiences. Teachers, therefore, need to be careful that other methods of certification, such as The Certificate of Achievement, Junior Sports Leaders Award or Hanson Award, are not ignored when they may actually be more enjoyable and relevant for many pupils. A Record of Achievement, for example, may be more appropriate for some pupils since it focuses on a pupil's personal and social qualities, which are not assessed via examination.

As examination physical education expanded, some writers raised a number of issues surrounding its development. Dickenson and Almond (1987), for example, questioned whether 'physical education' was an appropriate title for GCSE and 'A' level, given that it was also used in other contexts. More critically, they wondered whether examination courses in physical education were really necessary at all given the availability of sports studies, dance and outdoor pursuits examinations.

Arguments for Examinations in Physical Education

Attitudes towards formal assessment began to change in the 1980s. Whereas previously, physical educators and headteachers had seen extra-curricular sport as important as curriculum physical education, schools and individual subjects were becoming increasingly accountable under the Thatcher government's push for tests and examination results to be a top priority. Physical education needed to stay in line with these developments. The onset of GCSE not only gave physical education the credibility to stave off low status, but more critically to survive within an ever more competitive school timetable. The liberal arguments of education for its own intrinsic worth were dismissed in some quarters as lacking substance in the pragmatic and business-orientated educational system of the 1980s and 1990s. As Casbon (1988, p. 219) highlighted:

> The old argument that Physical Education is so intrinsically worthwhile that it does not need an examination does not stand up to any test in this new age of education. We are bound, as a profession, to have to be accountable in educational terms for what we teach.

The advent of GCSE and 'A' level physical education was taken as an opportunity to bolster the academic respectability of the subject. The theoretical dimension of GCSE physical education, which Aylett (1990) has suggested was made more difficult to compensate for the practical weighting of the course, meant that physical education could no longer be accused of lacking substance. Indeed, in the context of 'A' Level, Carroll (1994, p. 90) has suggested that 'the twin demands of breadth in terms of the range of disciplines and depth within each discipline are rarely demanded in one syllabus at this level'.

The theoretical content of examination physical education offered pupils excellent cross-curricular opportunities. Additionally, the distinctive character of physical education meant it appealed to many children in a way that other subjects did not. Helping otherwise disaffected pupils to do better in their examinations was a valuable service that physical education could provide, particularly in light of the growing importance of results. As examinations in physical education became more established, the subject could no longer be ignored. The more central function of a popular examination meant physical education could have a greater say in the running of the school and argue more forcibly for resources.

As the sport and physical recreation market expanded, and with it employment opportunities, it was felt important that sufficient young people became suitably qualified. Missing out as an examination subject would have deprived pupils of an opportunity to gain a worthwhile certificate that demonstrated their personal attributes and interest in a valued cultural domain. The argument went that pupils deserved the opportunity to do more than learn recreational forms of physical education, which, it was argued, did little to increase the profile of the subject. Examination physical education allowed pupils to take their knowledge and understanding further and to aim for higher standards. OfSTED (1995), for example, reported that the best work at Key Stage 4 was usually seen in examination classes.

Examinations also had benefits for teachers, who needed a new challenge and a focus for their professional development. Teaching examination classes offered physical educators a new perspective, and for many, classroom work meant that there was less need to move out of physical education to other responsibilities as their careers progressed. As Carroll (1994, p. 24) points out, examinations helped to give the physical educator 'more clarity of role'. Promotion was also at stake to some extent since a head of department, who had produced a successful GCSE or 'A' level programme, was more likely to stand comparison with peers for a senior management job.

Issues in Examination Physical Education

In order to conform to existing standards and expectations of examinable subjects, it was argued that a strong emphasis on theoretical assessment was necessary in physical education. Some physical educators felt that the subject already had a substantial body of knowledge closely related to physical performance. As Carroll (1994, p. 83) points out, 'there is no doubt that there is a great deal of knowledge in physical education which perhaps has always been undervalued but was worthy of inclusion in a course in which pupils were interested'. Therefore, by the mid-1990s, for example, each examination board at GCSE level included some aspect of safety and injury, anatomy and physiology, performance, and fitness and health (cf. Hodgson, 1996). Since these factors also allowed for written assessment, a compromise was reached between theory and practice in terms of course content.

At 'A' level, the academic nature of study meant that physical education required a very strong theoretical framework that fitted the ethos of further education, prepared candidates for university and would be comparable with other subjects. The various disciplines were, therefore, assessed through written work, and concentration on pupils' practical performance was rather marginalized. Despite this emphasis, though, there were predictable difficulties in the early stages of obtaining whole-hearted acceptance for 'A' level physical education by admissions tutors of higher education institutions (Francis, 1992).

The less tangible aspects of physical education, such as the processes associated with personal and social development, were difficult to measure in examination work (DES, 1989). Carroll (1994) has identified three main components of GCSE physical education: performance, knowledge and understanding, and analysis and evaluation, of which the first two came to dominate. This approach helped to ensure standardization, since it concentrated on the more concrete aspects of the subject, but at a possible risk of overlooking other traditional aspects of physical education.

Equity has been identified as an issue of concern within physical education examinations, as examinations are often used for selection purposes. Twice as many boys as girls take examinations in physical education (OfSTED, 1995), and this raises doubts that the subject is being presented in a way that is equally accessible to both boys and girls. There has been little work reported on pupils' reasons for choosing to do examination physical education, though the reasons are likely to be varied and complex. Roberts (1996) has postulated that teenage girls may simply like sport and physical education less than boys, but it seems that there is more to such under-representation than this alone. Examinations in physical education may reflect and reinforce gender stereotyping in physical education. This is clearly problematic and may be due to girls' perceptions of their ability and suitability to the subject and teacher selection processes (Carroll, 1998). Research by MacPhail (2000) into pupils' choices for Scottish Highers indicated that, in part, choice was due to the interest and enjoyment they had previously experienced in physical education lessons, as well as the relevance of the subject to future career aspirations.

It could also be that girls perceive the course structure, assessments and syllabi as inequitable. Certainly, Flintoff (1991) has expressed concerns over the appropriateness and equity of GCSE physical education practical work for girls. Specifically, she highlights the need to consider the complexities of sex and gender issues in examination courses, because 'important sex differences between boys and girls are largely ignored, and as a result, the examinations condone assessment procedures which are at best, inadequate, at worst discriminatory' (Flintoff, 1991, p. 35). Research suggests this issue still influences decision-making by pupils, and the poor performance of girls compared to their male counterparts 'raises significant questions in relation to the choice of syllabus and the selection of both appropriate and appealing activities' (Stidder, 2001, p. 33).

The different nature of sports and games is also problematic within the context of assessment. Although physical skills on the surface are the least controversial aspect of assessment, there can be certain idiosyncrasies. In activities like swimming and athletics, pupils can be assessed without reference to other children since the criteria for marks is set against times or distances. Such objectivity and reliability in criterion-referenced assessment is a lot more problematic in the open context of games. Here, individual performances depend on other pupils' responses, which provide a new set of difficulties for teacher assessment. For example, pupils' decision-making processes and tactical play can only be assessed in relation to team-mates and the opposition.

A further difficulty teachers face with criterion referencing is that variable conditions, such as playing surfaces and the weather, can drastically alter the environment, rendering the criteria and the norms they are based on somewhat uncertain. For example, pupils may find performance of some skills easier on an all-weather pitch than on grass or a pitted concrete surface. Similarly, sprinting on a rubber athletics track compared to grass can make a significant difference to times, which can be further affected by running in a strong wind. It will be important that schools do not rely on a one-off day of assessment where the elements seriously detract from pupil performance.

Implications for the Teacher

Physical education departments need to think carefully about delivering examination courses before they take on such a commitment. The considerable time and effort required in addition to the other demands placed on staff (e.g., development of the National Curriculum; commitment to extra-curricular sport) may significantly increase work loads, particularly if the department is relatively small. As Mackreth (1998, p. 17) has commented:

> Teachers perhaps have to be a little stronger when asked to implement 'A' Level, and more realistic as to the demands . . . One of these demands is obviously time, not only the time needed in delivering the course, but the time needed to set up, prepare and implement the course. Many head teachers underestimate both the time and work needed . . . Under resourcing is also another problem that centres face . . . there has to be a major financial input (of) books, periodicals, camcorder and video.

Choosing the most appropriate syllabus for pupils is a critical matter. Although there is a reasonable amount of similarity between the examination boards, subtle but important differences in format and structure of both content and assessment exist. These distinctions are clearly significant as a well-chosen course can emphasize pupils' particular strengths and abilities.

Since no two departments are the same (in terms of their philosophy, finance, timetable constraints, available facilities or staff expertise) the ability to deliver physical education will vary and this is likely to influence the choice of examination syllabus. In terms of choosing the right course, Scott (1997, p. 15) points out that there is 'no panacea, no one person has "the answer for everyone"'. The trick would seem to be to keep abreast of changes to the syllabi and to pick the course that best fits the distinctive needs of the school population, whilst also being deliverable. Teachers who are about to set up an examination course or change to a new examination board would be wise to consult with surrounding schools in order to compare the advantages and disadvantages of different syllabi.

Many schools find providing a GCSE course that enables pupils to take at least three activities from three of the six National Curriculum areas a major stumbling block (Scott, 1997). For these schools GCSE Physical Education (Games) provides a viable alternative, since it narrows the syllabus (although the manner in which the games are divided up can also present difficulties). At 'A' level, too:

> . . . teething problems (have emerged). Teachers have to come to terms with an expanded range of practical activities . . . This has created teachers with logistical problems in terms of time, facilities, staff expertise, and student expectations. There is no

one answer to the problem, with each Centre having to devise its own solution. (Mackreth, 1998, p. 17)

Furthermore, Carroll (1994) suggests that the strong discipline structure of 'A' level physical education disrupts the course and affects its cohesion.

Preparing pupils for examinations in physical education can begin during Key Stage 3 simply through good practice and linking the requirements of the National Curriculum to the examination syllabus. The effective teaching of fitness and health, such as utilizing warm-ups to familiarize pupils with relevant terminology and the identification of different muscles and how they work, can give pupils a reasonable understanding of some aspects of anatomy and physiology. Using teaching styles that encourage pupils to learn in different ways and in different contexts and thus prepare them for the demands of GCSE can also be valuable. For example, giving pupils the opportunity to analyse performance, or select and apply tactical strategies through indirect teaching methods, will lay the foundations for future assessments. Furthermore, the utilization of relevant visual displays can help to reinforce important examination information.

High achievement in examination physical education is more likely through a constructive partnership between pupils and teachers. 'A' level pupils can be involved in planning how they meet learning targets. This is particularly important where they are working towards National Curriculum Key Skills: candidates need to assume greater control over their learning, as they are responsible for creating a portfolio of evidence. According to Francis and Merrick (1994, p. 16) 'A' level teachers are becoming much more confident in the 'reciprocal teaching style being used in the practical programme (to produce) well-informed candidates who are able to express themselves authoritatively'.

Almost by their nature, the majority of 'A' level pupils are well motivated and have a mature attitude to learning. Teachers can thus act as facilitators, rather than merely curriculum deliverers (see Chapter 4). Pupils will need support in planning and structuring project work and in keeping to deadlines however. Teachers can support pupils to find the best ways of linking in National Curriculum Key Skills (e.g., Information Technology) so that it demonstrates their competence at the highest level possible. Effective guidance can ensure that more than one Key Skill is demonstrated in a suitably wide-ranging and co-ordinated project.

It is important that pupils know how assessment criteria are applied and how well they are doing so they can adjust their performances. Keeping pupils regularly informed of their assessment grades throughout the course can be an effective motivational tool as it often inspires them to further practice. Teachers can encourage pupils to attend extra-curricular clubs in order to improve their grades. Additionally, acclimatizing pupils to the formal, practical assessment situation can be beneficial, particularly where pupils lack confidence or are unused to performing under pressure.

Physical education has sometimes been seen as the repository for less able or disaffected pupils (Murphy, 1990). Since the success of a course can partially depend on the intake of pupils who select it, it will be worth fighting to ensure physical education is placed in an appropriate examination subject options group. A viable alternative for some schools may be compulsory GCSE as part of the 'core' physical education programme. This provides every pupil with certified evidence of their endeavour in physical education after two years without them having to opt for the subject in favour of another curriculum subject (cf. Stidder, 2000). Furthermore, the utilization of GCSE within 'core' physical education can be an excellent way to motivate pupils.

The unusually poor examination results of girls in physical education suggests that consideration of gender grouping policies may be required. Since boys can often dominate the physical education lesson and intimidate their female peers, single-sex examination classes may be an option. Where classes are mixed, teachers need to attend to possible gender issues. This will include ensuring girls are not disadvantaged by the practical activities offered. 'Sex fair' assessment procedures (Browne, 1988) also mean that girls are not unfairly compared to physically stronger boys. It is important that teachers do not let inaccurate, traditional images of what girls and boys can do affect their judgements.

Newly qualified teachers can be a great asset to a department in terms of delivering examination courses. They are usually very enthusiastic and their ebullient nature can often inspire the pupils they teach. More experienced colleagues can also benefit from newly qualified teachers who bring a fresh approach to the school, including innovative and enjoyable teaching methods to support pupils' learning. Furthermore, newly qualified teachers may have a high level of expertise in certain areas of the syllabus based on their degree or post-graduate work. For example, a sports science graduate is likely to have an in-depth knowledge of physiology.

Although newly qualified teachers are often keen to teach examination classes, it can be worth introducing them to this aspect of schooling gradually. There are many other professional issues to deal with in the first year or two of teaching (e.g., pastoral care, getting to know the school's routines, liaising with parents, etc.), so the responsibility of an examination group may be too much for the inexperienced teacher. The advent of league tables and inter-subject grade comparisons means examination work carries with it extra pressure and risk that may be better suited to more experienced colleagues.

The extensive content of examination courses, which have to be delivered in a set time, means that teachers needs to be highly efficient in their delivery. This can be a very challenging task for an inexperienced teacher. Trainee teachers are expected to gain experience of examination courses in their training. However, partnership-school availability and teachers' anxieties over letting trainees practise on their examination classes means many newly qualified teachers often lack the experience and confidence to teach examination courses. As Carroll (1994, p. 65) comments, 'specific expertise is required to devise suitable questions and mark schemes over and above the expertise in the subject'.

The pace of examination classes can be considerably quicker than other types of teaching so teachers will need additional information and easy access to practices and activities. They will also need to be flexible and adaptable to respond on a week-by-week basis to what happens in lessons. Planning and preparing individual lessons that follow on directly from previous experiences (often in a short time frame) is an advanced skill for which more experienced teachers are usually better equipped. Furthermore, the depth and wide-ranging nature of the syllabi (notably at 'A' level), means that physical educators can find themselves teaching or supervizing a topic that is unusual or unfamiliar to them. Such work can take a lot longer to prepare. The problem is sometimes accentuated by newly qualified teachers' lack of subject knowledge and the limited time available to them to develop the 'know how' to cope with advanced examination work.

Classrooms provide a new set of dynamics and problems with which the teacher will need to become familiar, and teaching the theoretical aspects of a course will be somewhat novel to the teacher more used to the sports hall or field. For example, breaking down complex theoretical material and presenting it in an interesting and enjoyable way can take a great deal of expertise. Presenting theoretical work in practical ways can be particularly important in terms of keeping pupils interested and engaged in learning.

It is important for teachers in the same department to standardize their assessments. Problems can occur with both experienced and inexperienced staff alike: 'experience of standardisation meetings . . . suggest that those teachers with a lot of expertise in a specific activity and who have been used to working at a high level can be harsh at GCSE marking in that particular activity . . .' (Carroll, 1994, p. 85). Departments can set up regular, informal, internal moderation of their marking and interpretation of the evidence, and share their judgements, in an attempt to bring about greater consistency and objectivity.

Observing pupils play sport and comparing them to a given criteria is open to accusations of subjectivity. However, the teacher's job has been made easier with regard to practical assessment because 'it has been shown through the GCSE that when criteria is made explicit, then assessment is reduced to much more of a technical exercise, which is open to standardisation and moderation' (Carroll, 1994, p. 16). Despite the use of explicit criteria, awarding grades is a sensitive and complex process, since it is not always obvious what a teacher should assess. Inexperienced teachers may also be unaware that they are assessing qualities in a pupil's performance other than those stated in the syllabus.

The acquisition of skill is not a unitary dimension; there are different levels of competence that have to be identified (Carroll, 1994). New teachers have to come to terms with such a system, and, as there is so much at stake, formal, summative, examination assessment can be a cause of anxiety. However, concentrating on end-of-topic or end-of-year assessments can be dangerous, since it implies that assessment is understood as a separate process from learning. It is important that teachers continuously diagnose pupils' work to help them improve, as well as using assessment to inform their own teaching and ensure that things are going to plan. Such advanced work takes time to develop, so the cut and thrust of examination courses may not be the ideal place for teachers to begin.

The extra pressure and work that teaching examination courses brings is something with which all new teachers have to deal, so the utilization of in-service training remains an important issue. Where possible, having an inexperienced physical educator firstly observe examination classes and then team-teach with an experienced practitioner would seem a sensible way forward. If a more established colleague shares a group with an inexperienced teacher, the former can monitor the group's progress whilst the latter can start by teaching elements of the syllabus and take on greater responsibility as time, competence and confidence permits. In England and Wales, the newly qualifed teacher can use the Career Entry Profile to target improvement in this area.

Conclusion

Examinations have helped to place physical education more centrally within the school. Their development, however, has not always been smooth. Examinations have meant physical educators have had to deal with a number of important and difficult issues over the last thirty years. However, in considering the place and content of examinations, teachers have also had to consider how they view physical education. Furthermore, examination courses have provided pupils with the opportunity to study the subject to a greater depth, and to use accreditation as a means to further study or employment.

CHAPTER 7

Special Educational Needs and Differentiation

Introduction

Teachers are finding themselves faced with increasing demands on their time and expertise. Some have expressed doubts that they are capable of meeting the needs of an increasingly diverse school population (Jenkinson, 1997). This feeling of powerless-ness may be even greater during physical education lessons, in which different special needs other than those that are routinely discussed may arise (Bailey and Robertson, 2000). The context for the discussion of these issues is that of educational policy in the United Kingdom which currently places a strong emphasis on the development of more inclusive provision and practice. At some level, at least, this policy seems to be based on values and beliefs that are associated with the concept of equality.

Political commitment to a more inclusive educational system is outlined in the government Green Paper, *Excellence for All Children: Meeting Special Educational Needs* (DfEE, 1997) and the consequent document *Meeting Special Educational Needs: a Programme of Action* (DfEE, 1998), which states:

> There are strong educational, as well as social and moral grounds for educating children with SEN, or with disabilities, with their peers. This is an important part of building an inclusive society. An increasing number of schools are showing

that an inclusive approach can reinforce a commitment to higher standards for all. (DfEE, 1998, p. 23)

This is really saying two things of great importance to teachers and policy-makers: first, that the inclusion of pupils with special needs has a moral as well as a practical dimension; second, that the effective development of such inclusive provision will be for the benefit of *all* pupils, not just those with special needs. As some writers have pointed out, such claims are not without their problems, not least because they are based upon an uncertain empirical base. Nevertheless, arguments for greater inclusion are influencing current educational practice both in the UK and abroad (Haug and Tossebro, 1998; Jenkinson, 1997), and as such, they demand consideration.

Questions of educational provision are often highly complex, and there are rarely simple solutions to difficult problems. Even if there were such solutions, it is by no means clear that their implementation into practice would be successful. The sort of changes to the educational system that are envisaged by some advocates of inclusive education are so profound that they would require a fundamental reconceptualization of the very aims of education, not just curriculum and pedagogy. The full implications of these changes for physical education have not yet been fully recognized, but they are likely to be quite far-reaching. Barton (1993, p. 49) has argued that physical education 'is the creation of an able-bodied people' and that it 'gives priority to certain types of human movement'. The motivation to participate in physical education, he argues, is encouraged through idealized notions of 'normality'. Criticisms of this kind have been raised in connection with gender (Talbot, 1996), but the case here seems even more persuasive, since a considerable amount of the mainstream curriculum is literally inaccessible to many disabled pupils.

Exclusive Physical Education

There is a huge body of evidence showing that physical activity is a vital component in the healthy development of all children (for example, see Bailey, 1999a; Malina and Bouchard, 1991). Regular and positive physical activity is a necessary condition of normal physical, emotional and social development. As the only formal exposure to physical activity that some pupils may have, a varied, positive physical education experience is essential. However, some authorities have raised doubts that pupils with certain impairments, especially those with more severe physical and learning disabilities, receive such an experience (Jowsey, 1992). Whether it is due to negative attitudes, poor training or lack of support, many teachers feel unprepared to deal with some pupils in their care.

All children require regular, quality physical education, and it may be that pupils with disabilities or learning difficulties require an even greater amount than their peers, as out-of-school opportunities for physical activity can be very restricted. Competence in physical skills and activities is a significant factor in pupils' experiences of school and their overall quality of life. Success in physical skills is seen by some pupils as more worthwhile than success in classroom-based activities, and participation in such activities is seen as a key factor in the development of social relationships and self-esteem (Bailey, 1999b). Unfortunately, many pupils with Special Educational Needs experience less physical activity than their peers (Brown and Gordon, 1987), and this seems to include those pupils without a disability related specifically to movement.

There is a danger that the child denied the opportunity of physical activity will suffer a number of disabling consequences. Aside from the well-established risks of low levels of activity (such as obesity, high blood pressure and weak bones), there are risks to the child's potential social and emotional health:

> To the degree that a child's activity pattern is distorted by impairment, socialisation occurs outside a normal context, and a child cannot fully gain the competencies required to dwell easily within the home, community, and society. (Brown and Gordon, 1987, p. 828)

There is a further risk that the difficulties experienced by a pupil with Special Educational Needs will develop into a 'spiral of failure', whereby early difficulties with activities lead to attempts to avoid those activities, which result in less practice, and so even greater difficulties (Ripley *et al.*, 1997).

From Special Education to Inclusive Education

> Inclusion is not about placing children in mainstream schools. It is about changing schools to make them more responsive to the needs of all children. It is about helping all teachers to accept responsibility for the learning of all children in their school and preparing them to teach those children who are currently excluded from their school, for whatever reason. (Mittler, 2000, pp. vii–viii)

The phrase 'Special Educational Need' originated in the late 1960s, as a response to an increasing dissatisfaction with the language of handicapping conditions, and a recognition that the system of segregated education was failing many pupils with physical or learning difficulties, both in their educational experience and their social and personal development (Oliver, 1996). The Warnock Report (DES, 1978) was an attempt to address these issues in the United Kingdom. It rejected the notion that there are two types of children: those with and those without a handicap. The nature of individual needs was recognized as far more complex than such a crude division implies. Whether an individual's condition constitutes an educational handicap depends upon many factors, such as the school's expertise and resources, the pupil's personality, the quality of support, and the encouragement within the family and community. It was considered entirely conceivable that a pupil with a disability could, in many contexts, perform as well or better than peers, given appropriate support. By focusing upon a pupil's 'need', rather than a 'handicap', the emphasis shifted from a mere description to a statement of the educational help and provision required.

The notion of Special Educational Needs has continued to receive endorsement through successive central policy documentation (in the United Kingdom, for example, through the Education Reform Act, 1988, and the Code of Practice, 1994). However, some people have raised concerns. Jean Gross (1996), for example, points out that a Special Educational Need was originally something a pupil *had in certain circumstances*, and perhaps for a certain period of time, while it has often come to mean something that a pupil *is*. Inflexible conceptions of Special Educational Needs prevent the teacher from fully understanding the particular needs of pupils, and can lead to a pessimistic approach towards pupils who are failing, thereby neglecting the real obstacles to achievement:

> This is more than an issue of 'politically correct' language. It is about the constant use of words that create or maintain mindsets that perpetuate segregation at the very time when we are talking about moving towards a more inclusive educational system and a more inclusive society. In this context, the continued use of 'special' is not only anachronistic but discriminatory. (Mittler, 2000, p. 8)

A number of recent debates in Special Education, especially those linked to calls for inclusion, seem to revolve around different concep-

The individual model	The social model
Personal tragedy theory	Social oppression theory
Personal problem	Social problem
Expertise	Experience
Adjustment	Affirmation
Attitudes	Behaviour
Care	Rights
Control	Choice
Individual adaptation	Social change

Table 7.1   *Disability models* (adapted from Oliver, 1996)

tions of disability. Oliver (1996) has been highly influential in positing a binary distinction between what he calls 'individual' and 'social' models of disability. A reliance upon the individual model, he argues, lies at the heart of inappropriate provision for disabled people. The 'problem' of disability, according to this model, is located within the individual, and the causes of this problem stem from some impairment or limitation which is assumed to arise from disability. Underpinning these assumptions is a view of disability as some personal tragedy. The social model, on the other hand, denies that individual limitations or losses are the causes of the problem. Rather, it is located within society, and its failure to meet the needs of a particular group. So the social model upholds the view that it is society which disables individuals, not any impairment they may have. By way of summary, Table 7.1 exemplifies the differences between the two models.

The traditional notion of special education, such as that promoted in the Warnock Report, has been criticized by many commentators as flawed, since it is grounded in the individual model (Booth, 1998). Corbett (1995, p. 15) is fairly representative when she writes that special educational needs is 'a redundant term, redolent with oblique undertones of exclusion and stigmatization'.

It is for these reasons, among others, that many educators and policy-makers have started to refer to Inclusive, rather than Special Education. This is more than a simple change in terminology, since it reflects a conviction that nothing short of a radical reappraisal of the structure and character of schooling is needed if it is to adequately meet the needs of all its pupils (cf. Jenkinson, 1997).

These views certainly have an important international reference point, The Salamanca Statement (UNESCO, 1994, p. 11):

> The fundamental principle of the inclusive school is that all children should learn together, wherever possible, regardless of any difficulties or differences they may have. Inclusive schools must recognise and respond to the diverse needs of their students, accommodating both different styles and rates of learning and ensuring quality education to all through appropriate curricula, organisational arrangements, teaching strategies, resource use and partnerships with their communities. There should be a continuum of special needs encountered by every school.

Here we see the expectation that education for all pupils, regardless of their differing abilities, will begin and continue in their local neighbourhood schools. In the UK, recent policy documents (DfEE, 1997; 1998) have signalled that inclusive educational policy development will have a prominent position for the foreseeable future.

Different Types of Needs

> Every man is in certain respects, a) like all other men; b) like some other men; c) like no other men. (Kluckholn *et al.*, cited in Norwich, 1990, p. 122)

The term Special Educational Needs, though it may be regarded as less disparaging and more educationally useful than those of earlier times (retardation, sub-normality, and so on) has significant limitations. In one sense, it is very vague, telling us little about the nature of difficulties experienced by a child. In another sense, it is unhelpfully stigmatizing, lumping many different pupils together as 'SEN', but failing to recognize individual differences or needs.

As was discussed above, some writers have associated the concept of Special Needs with the individual model of disability, and their rejection of one is linked to that of the other. Moreover, there is a tendency to adopt an either–or stance towards models of disability, so that either you are entirely in favour of the individual model, with its assumed emphasis upon defects and tragedy, or you are against it. But there is another view: these models are *not* mutually incompatible, as we need to think of them in a state of constant and complex interaction (Mittler, 2000). The individual model is premised on the need to find out as much as possible about a pupil's difficulties in order to plan an adequate educational intervention. The aim is to help the pupil benefit as much as possible from the school experience. The social model can be seen as a complimentary stance, premised on the need for society and the school to remove barriers to full participation of *all* pupils (Oliver, 1990).

Recent policy and theoretical developments (DfEE, 1998; Haug and Tossebro, 1998) suggest a movement away from the traditional individual model, and towards a social conception of ability and disability. However, there remains value in retaining an awareness of the effects of impairment upon an individual's performance. Within the context of physical education, for example, it is certainly the case that the profession needs to think seriously about the obstacles it has presented to pupils with disabilities that unnecessarily interfere with their access to meaningful movement experiences. At the same time, though, it would be foolhardy to underestimate the relevance of impairment or difficulty in relation to an individual's physical activity. What is needed, it seems, is an approach to inclusion that balances a recognition of the (removable) social and environmental barriers to participation with an awareness of the specific difficulties of individuals in a class.

Bailey and Robertson (2000) have proposed the adoption of an alternative model, based upon Norwich's (1996) triadic conception of pupil needs. According to this approach, needs can be understood in three ways, each of which interconnects with the others:

- *Individual Needs* – arising from characteristics different from all others.
- *Exceptional Needs* – arising from characteristics shared by some, such as Developmental Co-ordination Disorder, visual impairment, high ability.
- *Common Needs* – arising from characteristics common to all, such as the need to achieve, to play alongside other children, to belong.

This triadic model allows for a more complex and humane view of needs. It helps teachers to consider a range of needs and their educational implications, and it also ensures that a singular view of needs does not dominate. In physical education this would mean that an individual's particular difficulties, strengths and interests are given focused consideration. It would also mean that shared characteristics are taken account of when they are relevant. Underlying these considerations needs to be a more general reflection of the benefits available to *all* pupils from physical education: what are the contributions that physical education can offer to every pupil in the school? (See Chapter 1.)

When considering pupils with different needs and conditions, teachers always need to be ever-careful that they do not lose sight of that which is most important. It can be easy in our discussions of various conditions, disabilities and impairments to forget that we are dealing with children, with the same need as their peers – to be children (Robertson, 1999b). Children have an intrinsic need to experience what Bruner (1983, p. 121) calls the 'culture of childhood': to play, act and be included with their peers. For example, when teaching specific motor skills to a pupil with Down's Syndrome, it will be useful to become familiar with aspects of motor learning that such youngsters may find difficult or easy, and to utilize appropriate professional advice and research evidence. Doing this would also go some way to combating the fear and uncertainty that some teachers seem to feel when working with pupils with physical and learning difficulties. This would ensure that teaching is optimally informed, and likely to be most effective. This is not the same as working with crude assumptions such as 'all Down's Syndrome children are . . .'. Moreover, the use of the typology of needs outlined above would enable a teacher to keep in focus the important inclusive imperative – that children have the right to learn together. In practice, this typology should be used flexibly, enabling particular needs to be addressed as priorities. Clearly, too, the three kinds of needs outlined here are not incompatible, and can be addressed simultaneously.

An associated issue, in this regard, relates to teachers' expectations of pupils' abilities. Teachers' attitudes towards their pupils can have a considerable effect on their behaviour towards those pupils, and this in turn influences the pupils' behaviours and attitudes to physical education. Rink (1993, p. 47) calls these 'expectancy effects', and they can easily result in the development of the 'spiral of failure' described earlier. There is considerable evidence that many teachers have unwarranted low expectations of pupils with special educational needs, of whatever type (Kaplan, 1996). Moreover, very able pupils are given more opportunities to interact with the teacher than low achievers (Cohen *et al.*, 1996). These expectations can have both indirect and direct effects on pupils' learning. Indirectly, low teacher expectation may lead some pupils to modify their perception of their own ability, which may influence the goals they set themselves and the standards with which they are satisfied. More directly, well-meaning teachers may actually restrict the learning opportunities they offer some pupils.

The triadic view of pupils' needs also allows for the possibility that biological, psychological and social factors can interact to both cause and ameliorate a child's learning difficulties (Cooper, 1996). Knowing about these factors can be very useful in considering how best to meet a pupil's needs in physical education. In this regard, Sugden and Wright (1996) have proposed a simple framework for identifying pupils with special needs in physical education. They distinguish between pupils who have a need which is *primarily described in terms of their movement skills* (such as physical disabilities and movement difficulties), and those who have a need in physical education, but which is *secondary to other needs* (including learning difficulties, hearing and visual impairment, behavioural problems). This is not a strict and precise division, and not every pupil in these groups will have difficulties in physical education. Nevertheless, it serves to emphasize the needs that may arise in the specific context of a physical education lesson.

Moving Towards Inclusion

There remains a danger of 'medicalizing' (Oliver, 1990) special needs, through which teachers come to conceive of conditions purely in terms of clinical intervention. Of course, it is important to be aware of the character and implications of different needs in order to adapt the teaching and the curriculum appropriately, but this does not reduce or alter the vital educational role of the physical education teacher: 'a child with myopia is the responsibility of an eye doctor who prescribes lenses which are necessary for learning, but this does not diminish the responsibility of the teacher' (Norwich, 1999, p. 92). Norwich's quote highlights two related issues. First, that whatever the special need, the teacher always has a central role to play in educational decisions. Second, that an integrated approach to addressing the needs of children is of utmost importance. Different professionals have different expertise, and an adequate approach must recognize the roles that each can play. Teachers may need to access advice and guidance regarding certain aspects of a medical condition or physical impairment, but it needs to be remembered that clinicians and psychologists are not experts in classroom practice, nor in the delivery of physical education lessons.

There is another danger in this regard, and that is of believing that teaching pupils with special needs is of a different character to teaching other pupils. Whilst there are important aspects of a pupil's need that should be considered, the fundamental principles of teaching and curricular design remain the same. A brief consideration of the implications for teaching of various conditions reveals that almost all apply to all pupils – clarity of expectations; sensitive differentiation; careful assessment; identification of strengths as well as weaknesses; and so on (cf. Jowsey, 1992). Some may simply require greater emphasis in particular situations. There are circumstances in which it is important to develop knowledge and expertise that goes beyond general good practice, and this may involve the teacher seeking specialist help or engaging in some form of continuing professional development. However, this is not 'high specialism' (Robertson, 1999a, p. 78), associated with working in clinical settings. It is knowledge supporting good generic practice. The central point, however, is that,

> Teaching is teaching, regardless of the range of needs of pupils, and an essential prerequisite of integration in the new sense of the word is the acquisition of a commitment on the part of teachers to work with all children, whether they have special needs or not. (Oliver, 1996, p. 87)

In fact, it may be that mainstream physical education teachers are in the best position to work with pupils, especially with regard to initial learning, in which enthusiasm and making learning fun are more important factors of teaching than those which emphasize particular skills and techniques (Bloom, 1985). Moreover, as was discussed at the beginning of this chapter, a child's primary need is to be a child, and to be *with* other children. Physical education offers a distinctive and unequalled opportunity to address this need.

Changing Teaching and Learning in Physical Education

What does this mean for physical education? Certainly, there will be a need for innovative and creative thinking on the part of teachers. Blamires (1999) has argued that inclusion is fundamentally concerned with access and engagement with one's peers in tasks that are at an appropriate level and worthwhile. In practice, this seems most likely to occur when teachers and schools interpret their role with versatility, offering a range of provision, to meet the range of needs of their pupils.

Four principles have been proposed to inform the planning and content of physical education for *all* pupils (DES/WO, 1992; see also Vickerman, 1997):

- *Entitlement* – all pupils have a right to fully participate in worthwhile activities.
- *Access* – which is achieved primarily by the provision of appropriate and challenging learning experiences and assessment mechanisms, allowing for modification when required.
- *Integration* – pupils, even when following an adapted curriculum, should be doing so alongside their peers.
- *Integrity* – physical education lessons should be demanding, motivating and exciting educationally.

According to this model, physical education needs to strike a balance between challenge and flexibility; between presenting pupils with sufficiently demanding activities and modifying those activities to reflect their individual needs and abilities. At the same time, it stresses a central principle of an inclusive physical education: wherever possible, pupils should learn together.

Bailey and Robertson (2000) highlight two consequences of a properly inclusive approach to physical education. First, teaching practices will need reshaping. Second, the organization of learning will have to become infinitely more flexible than it is at present. This implies a radical rethinking on the part of physical educators in the coming years. It also implies that differentiated practice will need to become much more central to teaching and learning.

Differentiation

Special needs teaching is not something different and distinct from other forms of teaching, but as an extension of good professional practice. (Sugden and Wright, 1996, p. 121)

Teaching pupils with special needs or disabilities is not of a different character to teaching other pupils. While there are important aspects of pupils' needs that should be considered in planning and teaching, the basic principles of good practice outlined in this book are the same for all pupils, although some aspects may require greater emphasis in certain situations.

Effective teaching requires that a range of teaching strategies, tasks and forms of organization are used to meet the different needs of the pupils in a class. This is often referred to as 'differentiation', and it constitutes one of the most valuable skills a teacher can acquire and develop. Differentiation involves 'recognising the variety of needs within a class, planning to meet needs, providing appropriate delivery and evaluation of the effectiveness of the activities in order to maximise the achievements of individual students' (NCET, 1993, p. 21).

According to inspection reports, differentiation is a particular weakness of newly qualified teachers. Her Majesty's Inspectorate (DES, 1988, p. 22) claimed that even in 'good' and 'excellent' lessons observed, there were still occasional weaknesses in 'differentiating the work so as to match the different levels of ability among pupils'. Similarly, OfSTED (1995a, p. 24) reported that 'a lack of adequate differentiation was a feature in many lessons observed'.

The key to effective differentiation is planning (see Chapter 3). The difficulty for the teacher working with an unfamiliar class is often a lack of knowledge of the range of abilities of the pupils. This can be addressed, to some extent, by talking to previous teachers of the classes to be taught, and through looking at pupils' assessment files. There may be more information available on pupils with identified special needs. Ultimately, though, teachers need to make their own judgements about classes, and this comes from the experience of working with those classes. A useful approach during early lessons is to begin with tasks that are likely to challenge the majority of pupils, but also plan adaptations to those tasks for higher and lower abilities, and intervene with them if it becomes clear that certain pupils need a different level of challenge. Increased familiarity with a class allows for more precise planning and differentiation, so effective assessment strategies are essential (see Chapter 5).

Perhaps the simplest approach to differentiation is to distinguish between differentiation by task and outcome. *Differentiation by task* occurs when the teacher plans and presents a number of different tasks of varying difficulty, and the pupils choose or are directed to the task that matches their ability level. *Differentiation by outcome* occurs when the teacher sets a challenge, and the pupils each answer that challenge according to their individual levels of ability (see Table 7.2).

Whilst this categorization is quite clear and simple, it is far too general to provide sufficient support for good teaching in physical education. A more systematic approach is required.

A framework for making decisions about planning was introduced in the planning chapter. According to this model, the teacher makes a series of decisions that determine the character of the lesson. Each of the variables – organization, presentation and content – relates to a different aspect of the lesson. These variables can be further subdivided to offer a range of differentiation strategies. These strategies need not involve a great deal of extra work for teachers. In fact, they

Pupils plan and perform a gymnastic sequence in which weight must be taken on different body parts	Differentiation by task	• Using large body parts • Using stable bases (e.g., two feet and one hand) • Unstable bases (e.g., two hands) • Inverted (e.g., bunny hop or shoulder stand or handstand)
	Differentiation by outcome	• More challenging balances • Clear shapes/better body awareness • Variety of balances • Greater control

Table 7.2 *Differentiation by task and outcome* (adapted from CCW, 1992)

are just the decisions a teacher must make in the planning of any lesson. The advantage of the approach suggested here is that these decisions are made explicitly and in a systematic manner. By making decisions in this way, the teacher is in a position to differentiate to meet the needs of individuals or groups within a class (see Figure 7.1).

Differentiation by organization

Differentiation by grouping
There are many ways of organizing pupils into groups, such as ability, friendship or random groups. Generally, the smaller the group size, the easier it is for pupils to deal with the intellectual challenges presented to them: larger groups mean more choices and more decisions. When pupils are introduced to a skill or concept, it is often beneficial to allow them to work alone or in pairs as this can present less pressure, and give them greater opportunity to come to terms with the new knowledge and skills. As skills and understanding progress, pupils are better able to deal with the challenges presented by large groupings.

Differentiation by space
Altering the amount of space pupils have to work in can make performance of a task harder or less difficult. Pupils with certain special needs, for example those using a wheelchair, may need more space to be able to participate safely because turning can take longer. Increasing the size of a court gives the players more time to think

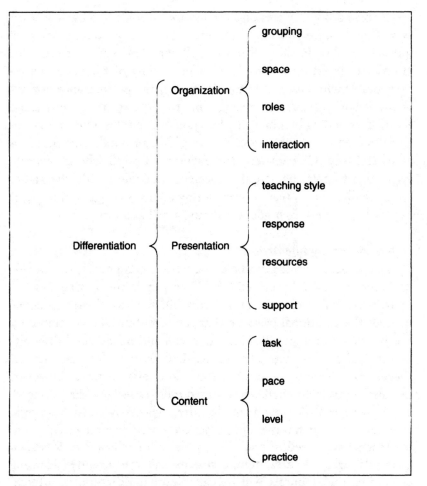

Figure 7.1   *Approaches to differentiation in physical education*

and act. Decreasing the space makes the game quicker and potentially more challenging. In gymnastics, asking the most able pupils to perform a gymnastics sequence within a smaller performance area than peers challenges them to develop their techniques and devise more imaginative sequences. It is also possible to divide up a playing area, and to restrict some players' movements around a court (as in netball). Specifying zones within which pupils must work makes decision-making easier, as well as preventing a small number of players dominating the game.

Differentiation by roles

Pupils can take a number of different roles within the activities of physical education. A game of rounders serves as a good example: it can involve a bowler, a back-stop and many fielders, a batting team as well as umpires, coaches, a scorer and even a commentator or sports journalist. Ideally, all pupils will experience each of the roles in order to build up a complete understanding of the game. However, pupils who are unable to take part in the performance aspects of the lesson (because of injury) can still develop their knowledge and understanding by practising less/non-active roles. Differentiation by roles is an excellent way of ensuring that all pupils take part in a *purposeful* way. One strategy for including a pupil who is severely disabled is to give that pupil a specific, vital role within the game. For example, once a team scores during an invasion game, the pupil can try to 'convert' that goal by aiming a ball at a target.

Differentiation by interaction
Physical education tasks can be co-operative, competitive or individual (Johnson and Johnson, 1975). When pupils are starting to learn a particular skill, it can often be worthwhile to allow them to practise without the additional pressure that can sometimes be generated by competition. Some pupils with emotional and behavioural difficulties can find competitive activities particularly stressful, and this can trigger misbehaviour or disaffection. Co-operative tasks, however, can also be used to challenge other pupils, especially the young or pupils with autistic spectrum disorder, who may need a gradual introduction to such forms of interaction. At the planning stage then, the teacher will need to consider a number of relevant factors such as pupils' ages, abilities, temperaments and the intended learning objectives. Older pupils will be capable of fairly complex interactions, and the teacher can draw on this competence to develop pupil learning, for example, pupils can plan out and lead their peers in health-related exercises.

Differentiation by presentation
This section refers to the way in which the curriculum can be presented to support pupils' learning and how they, in turn, demonstrate their skill, knowledge and understanding.

Differentiation by teaching style
Different learning outcomes demand different teaching styles. The introduction of a specific skill, particularly where there is a safety issue involved, means a direct style is likely to be most appropriate (e.g., a javelin lesson). Similarly, there will be times when pupils cannot be allowed to just 'have a go' because of the inherent danger

of the activity (e.g., handspring vault), so the teacher will have to instruct more directly. Conversely, where the teacher wants pupils to reflect on their performances or to consider a range of possible courses of actions, then indirect styles may be more relevant. It is important to note that as pupils have their own preferred learning styles, they will respond better to some styles of teaching than others: teachers will therefore have to be flexible in differentiating between different groups of pupils. Of course, teaching styles can be used to challenge pupils differently: more able pupils can be asked to discover a series of solutions to break down an opposition's tight defensive unit (divergent discovery), whereas less able pupils may need to be guided by a set of clues to reach the same objective. (These issues are discussed in greater depth in Chapter 4.)

Differentiation by response
There are various ways in which pupils can demonstrate their knowledge and understanding, such as through their actions, words or written communication, either as individuals, with a partner or as part of a group. The distinctively public nature of physical education means that some pupils can feel uncomfortable demonstrating their skills, but may be perfectly happy to explain their ideas to the teacher. Others may be happier showing their progress through performing either next to others or as part of a group rather than on their own.

Differentiation by resources
The effective use of resources is a necessary element in supporting learning. Changing resources can increase the difficulty of a task, or make it much easier to do. For example, a pupil with movement difficulties might start practising with a balloon instead of a volleyball because it will travel slower, making tracking more manageable. An able gymnast who has been working on the floor can be challenged by practising the skill on ever smaller pieces of apparatus. There are many different ways of varying the use of resources to meet the needs of pupils (the decision being made either by the teacher or the pupil), such as:

- Tempo, cadence and rhythm of music in dance classes.
- Size, weight, colour and texture of ball; size of bat/racquet; height of net; size of target/goal; length of handle; stationary or moving target in games.
- Height and or area of apparatus in gymnastics.

- Use of floats and other buoyancy aids in swimming and life-saving.

Differentiation by support

Teachers can choose to use their time and that of any other adult helpers available in different ways. Sometimes additional help is needed for specific activities, as when giving support in gymnastics. At other times, individuals or groups may benefit from extra attention from the teacher, or from focused monitoring. This is particularly possible when teachers combine differentiation by support with differentiation by resources: they can set certain pupils some purposeful and imaginative tasks using work cards or visual aids releasing themselves to concentrate on pupils working at a different level. Some pupils with a statemented special need may have a designated non-teaching assistant to support them, and teachers need to plan for these assistants' time, as well as their own.

Content variables

This relates to activities and tasks that are developed during a lesson.

Differentiation by task

A common form of differentiation is to plan different tasks (or different versions of the same task) to match pupils' abilities or needs.

Differentiation by pace

Pupils' different strengths and weaknesses, motivations and experiences are likely to mean that they progress through planned activities at different rates. By providing the class with a set of work cards that detail the different tasks of the lesson, pupils can progress through the tasks at their own speed: the most able are not held back and pupils who need more time are not rushed through. Another approach is to group pupils according to ability or fitness, extending the challenges presented to the more able or fitter groups, and giving more time for the less able groups.

Differentiation by level

Differentiation by level is a useful approach for the teacher to develop as it presents different levels of challenge for essentially the same task. This means the teacher can keep the class together whilst allowing everyone to work at a suitable level. For an inexperienced teacher or a teacher who is less confident in an activity, this can be advantageous. For example, in athletic activities an able group can be challenged to perform a full relay changeover at high speed, whereas another group could do a simplified version at lower speed. Similarly, gymnastics skills can be performed with different levels of difficulty (e.g., headstand in crouch for beginners, headstand in pike for the better gymnasts), and games can be played with different sizes of teams or teams of unequal size. In each case, the differentiation takes place through the level of challenge presented to pupils.

Differentiation by practice style
Many physical education activities can be taught as a whole or by being broken down into parts. Some pupils will prefer the latter whilst others may initially want to attempt parts of the whole. The basketball lay-up serves as a good example: the shot can be practised as one continuous action; or it can be broken down into three parts, a run-up, a jump and a shot. Pupils at different stages of skill development need different types of practice. Those who have recently acquired the skill may benefit from small, repeated drills, those developing fluency may need sustained practice, and those with a high level of skill may need to use the skill in an increasingly wider range of contexts. Table 7.3 presents a summary of the differentiation strategies, with examples of their application in physical education.

Organizing the Inclusive Lesson
Inclusive practices in physical education do not demand that all pupils participate at all times alongside their peers. Rather, it suggests that pupils should be included in lessons *as far as is possible and in their best interests*. The key here is flexibility of approach. Black and Haskins (1996) have proposed an 'inclusion spectrum' methodology in addressing pupils' different needs in physical education. According to this view, there are five different approaches to the delivery and organization of an activity: separate, adapted, parallel, modified and mainstream (see Figure 7.2).

Mainstream activities are those in which everyone in the class is included, without adapting or modifying the activity.

Modified activities involve the sorts of differentiation strategies discussed in the previous section – differentiated rules, space, equipment, roles and so on. Whilst there is differentiated or modified performance for pupils with different needs, all pupils work together on the same general task in the same area.

Parallel activities are those in which pupils of different abilities are

Strategy	Application
Differentiation by grouping	Swimming: pupils are divided in four groups by ability; non-swimmers remain in the shallow end of the pool; higher ability pupils use a lane for distance practice.
Differentiation by space	Games: pupils using wheelchairs are given more space in a passing game, to allow for the greater area needed to turn and move.
Differentiation by roles	Outdoor and adventurous activities: for a problem-solving task, one pupil in a group directs, another is the judge and two others carry out the physical challenge. They then rotate roles.
Differentiation by interaction	Tennis: pupils new to the sport practise ball control skills individually, then build up rallies co-operatively, before playing a simple competitive game.
Differentiation by teaching style	Dance: very able pupils are encouraged to explore different ways of using stimuli for movement.
Differentiation by response	Gymnastics: injured pupil uses ICT to plan and represent a sequence of basic actions and linking actions.
Differentiation by resources	Softball: pupils are allowed to choose the size of bat, and to select whether to hit a moving or stationary ball.
Differentiation by support	Athletics: a pupil with a visual impairment runs with a partner.
Differentiation by task	Dance: groups prepare a dance using different stimuli, such as music, poetry or natural sounds.
Differentiation by pace	Outdoor and adventurous activities: groups work through a series of tasks at their own rate.
Differentiation by level	Gymnastics: pupils perform headstand, with either tucked, straight or spread legs.
Differentiation by practice style	Games: less able pupils practise short, repeated tasks, whilst the most able group learn to adapt and generalize the skills in new contexts.

Table 7.3 *Differentiation strategies, with examples of application* (from Bailey, 2001a)

Mainstream activities	Modified activities	Parallel activities	Adapted activities	Separate activities
Total inclusion of all pupils	Differentiated rules, space, equipment, roles	Same game, ability grouping	All pupils play adapted game	Pupils play separately

Figure 7.2   *The inclusion spectrum* (based on Black and Haskins, 1996)

grouped together, and participate in their own way, but in the same task. For example, able-bodied and wheelchair-users might form two groups for games of volleyball.

Adapted activities occur when all pupils take part in adapted tasks, or tasks that are specifically designed with disabled people in mind. For example, all pupils might play Boccia (an aiming game, rather like French Petanque or Bowls) together.

Separate activities take place when a specific group of pupils practise an activity on their own. This might be in preparation for a competition, or for a movement assessment.

This approach offers the teacher a degree of flexibility in the organization of a lesson. For example, different parts of the lesson might be made up with mainstream and separate activities, or the whole class can progress through each of the approaches in turn (Black, 1999). The approaches used will depend upon a range of factors, such as the task being undertaken, the ability level and range of the pupils, and the learning objectives of the lesson. Whatever approach is adopted, it is important not to be dogmatic about its use. There is no correct way, in absolute terms, only more or less appropriate ways in specific situations. The goal of inclusive practice is to meet the needs of all pupils. A flexible use of a range of strategies increases the likelihood that all pupils will be challenged and motivated, and that none will feel excluded from physical education.

Assessment and Differentiation

The benefits of early identification assessment of Special Educational Needs are well established, and physical educators are likely to have access to types of information about pupils that are not available to other teachers. The nature of the subject means that physical education teachers may be the first professionals to gather certain sorts of information, such as:

- Movement difficulties.
- Emotional and behavioural difficulties associated with an inability to handle competitive stress, accidental physical contact, failure and success.

Other information may be more readily identifiable within the peculiar contexts of physical education, where they may have remained hidden elsewhere, including:

- Hearing and visual impairments.
- Social isolation.
- Language difficulties.
- Signs of physical abuse.

The 1993 Education Act, and the subsequent 'Code of Practice on the Identification and Assessment of Special Educational Needs' (DFE, 1994), provides a detailed and systematic framework for identifying, assessing, planning and monitoring Special Educational Needs. At the centre of the Code of Practice is a five-stage procedure, of which the first three stages relate to the school's internal procedures, and the last two to those of the Local Educational Authority (LEA). The end result of the five-stage process is usually the issuing of a 'statement of special educational needs' for the pupil, accompanied by some extra resources.

The five stages of the Code of Practice are outlined below:

Stage One is the teacher's responsibility, and involves an initial statement of concern that a pupil is experiencing some difficulties in mainstream provision. At this stage, the action will usually involve an assessment by the teacher, and, perhaps, an increase in the degree of differentiation offered. The teacher needs to pass the pupil's name to the school Special Educational Needs Co-ordinator (SENCO), who may decide to contact the parents, and who will review, with the teacher, the progress made by the pupil under the adapted provision.

Stage Two is the joint responsibility of the teacher and the SENCO, and requires the formulation of an Individual Education Plan (IEP), which describes in some detail the type of special need and the strategies being used to meet that need. The SENCO will work alongside the teacher, and together they will initiate a more detailed assessment of the pupil's needs to help with effective planning for that pupil. Progress will be reviewed, and a decision will be made regarding whether the pupil should remain at Stage

Two, or has made sufficient progress to return to Stage One, or to move to Stage Three.

Stage Three is mainly the responsibility of the SENCO, along with professionals from other agencies, such as educational psychologists, physiotherapists or GPs. A more thorough assessment of the pupil's needs will be carried out, and the SENCO will liaise closely with the teacher and parents to share information about the pupil's progress.

Stage Four is the school and LEA's responsibility. Reports from a range of interested parties (school, parents, educational psychologists, physiotherapists, social services, and so on) may be requested by the LEA. Formal assessment of the pupil's needs is begun, and this may result in the issuing of a 'statement', and with it greater resource support for the pupil.

Stage Five is the final phase of the procedure, and only relates to pupils with the most demanding special needs. At this stage, the LEA issues a statement, as well as extra money to the pupil. The school then has to implement the extra support and resources needed, as dictated by the statement. This is often in the form of a non-teaching assistant, or some specialist equipment. There are clear implications for the physical education teacher in planning for and working with this extra level of assistance.

Conclusion

This chapter has discussed three related concepts: special educational needs, inclusion and differentiation. It has suggested that teaching pupils with special needs is not of a different character to teaching any other pupils. While there are important aspects of an individual's needs that demand attention, the basic principles of teaching and curriculum design remain the same. This assertion lies at the heart of the call for inclusive practices in schools. Differentiation is a vital skill for all teachers, and it forms the central strategy for ensuring that all pupils receive a worthwhile, meaningful and challenging physical education. The strategies discussed here apply with equal force when working with disabled pupils, or with the very able. Good teaching is good teaching, and physical education teachers need to recognize the distinctive and essential contribution that their subject can make to *all* pupils, irrespective of ability.

CHAPTER 8

Talented Pupils in Physical Education

Introduction

Despite many people's devotion to sport in this country, and the wish for successful national sporting teams, research into talent identification in physical education has received comparatively little attention. Perhaps this is because of the 'public's misconception of the educational opportunities for (talented) children, and the difficulties in encouraging people to consider education for (talented) children as a priority when the need for other types of special education services is so much more visible' (Kaplan, 1996, p. 408). Yet, identifying the most able pupils to ensure they receive the appropriate level of challenge is clearly important, primarily for the pupils' educational opportunities and second for the nation's future sporting hopes. The education of highly able pupils is complicated, and the realization of excellence from childhood potential is subject to a complex blend of circumstance involving parents/carers, teachers, coaches, internal factors (e.g., motivation; interest), chance and the school learning environment.

Teaching a talented pupil can be a very challenging experience for the physical educator, so it is not difficult to understand why teachers may be uneasy about the practicalities of having such a pupil in their group. As Leyden (1990, p. 55) points out: 'a very able pupil . . . may have progressed beyond the competence of the teacher . . . (who) may be hard put to know how to present interesting and challenging problems.' Perhaps the biggest problem talented children face is the mistaken belief that, because of their high ability, they can look after themselves, and require less teaching than their peers. Ethically, too, teachers may feel they should spend more time with less able pupils: HMI (1993) found that some teachers felt it appropriate to overlook the most able in favour of helping the less able. Indeed, according to Maltby (1984), some teachers believed that resources were better spent on the less able.

In this light it is perhaps not surprising to find that several inspection reports have indicated that, in general, talented pupils are not sufficiently challenged (HMI, 1992; OfSTED, 2001). Inappropriate teaching inevitably reduces pupil motivation, can lead to a rejection of schooling and is clearly wasteful of pupils' time. Hildreth (1966, p. 531) has suggested that teachers will need to 'go beyond the text book in directing the (talented) in their studies', whilst Marjoran (1988) adds that teaching may need to be unorthodox! Indeed, some writers have suggested that very able pupils have a special need (Kaplan, 1996; Van Tassel-Baska, 1994). Glass *et al.*, (1982) have defined the most able in terms of provision, suggesting that the most able pupils are those who require some degree of modification in their educational programmes.

Interestingly, however, the influential Warnock Report (DES, 1978) on Special Educational Needs did not consider giftedness to be part of its remit. Likewise, although the Code of Practice on the Identification and Assessment of Special Educational Needs (DFE, 1994) recognized that there was a continuum of needs and a continuum of provision, it did not discuss very high ability as a special need.

The aim of this chapter is to provide a clearer picture of the nature of, and provision for, talented pupils in physical education. Inevitably, when research and understanding are not far advanced, as is the case here, a chapter like this can throw up as many questions as answers. However, it utilizes relevant general research to outline the key issues surrounding the education of talented children in physical education.

Gifted, Talented or Something Else?

Throughout history, the meaning of giftedness has varied, as it still does between different societies, according to the conceptions of the people who use the term. This means that giftedness cannot be viewed as excellence per se, but is always a relative matter – a function of circumstance, time and culture. (Freeman, 1983, p. 20)

The manner in which talent is defined is of vital importance, as definitions can influence the way people interpret the world and thus how policies are constructed. As Barton (1993, p. 43) has stated, 'definitions are crucial in that the presuppositions informing them can be the basis of stereotyping and stigmatisation'. The danger of creating an image or template of an able pupil is that although some children will be included, many who do not fit the stated characteristics will be excluded. This means that some children will not get the appropriate level of challenge that they deserve. The second danger for physical educators is that talent characteristically produces innovative behaviours. Imagine the prospect of discounting a junior Michael Johnson because of his strange running technique or telling Dick Fosbury to high jump properly!

Traditionally, schools only used formal Intelligent Quotient (IQ) measures to identify their most able children. However, it became apparent that the use of IQ scores was simply too restrictive to be representative of the wide variety of children's special talents. More recently definitions have broadened from the original notion of intellectual achievement, and there is now a multiplicity of measures that recognize the multiple talents that children possess.

Gardner's (1983) 'Theory of Multiple Intelligence' suggested a new approach in the development of a broader remit of high ability. He proposed that human abilities are best considered as a number of distinct *intelligences*, including musical, linguistic, logical-mathematical, spatial, interpersonal, intrapersonal and bodily-kinaesthetic. The last form of intelligence clearly relates closely to ability in physical education, representing a capacity for mind–body interaction and control. An alternative model is that of Gagne (1985), who proposed five general ability domains, including sensori-motor. Tannenbaum (1993) highlighted 'creativity' (innovation or invention; a novel response that solves the problem at hand) as representing a distinct aspect of giftedness, which is also pertinent to parts of physical education.

Teachers often talk of pupils in their class as being 'gifted'. However, Montgomery (1996) considers the term to be outmoded in present society, suggesting 'highly able' as a more appropriate substitute. Kaplan (1996) points out a recent trend to use the term 'prodigy' to define the child who can function at the level of a highly trained adult. Eyre (1994) has argued for the term 'exceptional ability', though Freeman (1998) has suggested that since the term 'gifted' is still used by most international researchers it seems sensible to stick with it. She further suggests that children's giftedness is usually seen in terms of preciousness compared with others of the same age. More specifically, this means 'a pupil or youth who performs at or shows potential for performing at a remarkably high level of accomplishment when compared to others of the same age, experience, or environment' (Sayler, 1999).

The multitude of definitions and different adjectives ('exceptional', 'most able', 'high ability') to describe the same phenomena, in subjects as diverse as physical education and mathematics, has been somewhat confusing and led the government to address the situation. The 'Excellence in Cities' project (DfEE, 2001) makes a clear distinction between physical education, art and music and the other statutory curriculum subjects. In the case of the three named subjects the most able pupils are to be identified as 'talented', whilst for the other subjects (mathematics, history and so on) 'gifted' is the suggested term. It is not clear why this distinction needs to be made: it may be due to a perception that the distinct performative elements within physical education, art and music warrant a different label for high ability; or it may be that there is an implicit hierarchy, in which some sorts of ability are more valued than others. Under these definitions, only 5–10 per cent of each year group in any school across all subjects are considered as gifted and talented (in total), reflecting the rare nature of these pupils. Indeed, Ashby (cited in Young and Tyre, 1992, p. ix) has called them 'the thin, clear stream of excellence'. International consensus tends to put the figure around the top 2–5 per cent of the pupil population (e.g., Tannenbaum, 1993).

Realistically, this means that there is not likely to be more than two or three talented pupils in physical education in a typical six or eight-form entry. For the sake of consistency with this current school guidance, the term 'talented' will be used in this chapter to identify this very small group of pupils. However, it should be recognized that there is another, larger group of pupils whose ability in physical education warrants special attention. Hildreth (1966), Renzulli and Reis (1991) and HMI (1993) suggest that around 15–20 per cent of pupils may be highly able. Although there is presently very limited guidance on the identification of talent in physical education, given the wide range of experiences and activity areas encompassed within the subject, it seems reasonable to suppose that between 10 and 15 per cent of pupils are of such high ability. This larger group will be referred to in this chapter as 'very able' pupils. Whilst these pupils may not exhibit the extraordinary ability of talented pupils, they nevertheless do seem to have an educational need that requires some form of differentiated provision. This chapter primarily concerns itself with talented pupils, but many of the principles outlined may be appropriate for the wider group.

The determination of talent in physical education is made very difficult owing to definitional problems, the diverse nature of the activities and the wide set of physical and mental characteristics required to excel in even one aspect of physical education. As Williams and Reilly (2000, p. 658) highlight, 'there is no consensus of opinion regarding the theory and practice of talent identification . . .'. Should talent imply a pupil who learns new techniques very quickly across a range of activities? Or does it refer to someone who demonstrates very high technical expertise? Or is a talented pupil one who exhibits great tactical understanding in games? What about a young dancer whose work shows great empathy, originality and creativity? Or is it the pupil who demonstrates remarkable leadership qualities? All of them could be identified as talented, suggesting a broad, generic definition of high ability is most appropriate for physical education to prevent certain pupils being excluded. In England and Wales, the National Curriculum (DfEE/ QCA, 1999) End of Key Stage Levels includes an 'Exceptional Performance' statement that has adopted such a pragmatic approach:

> Pupils consistently use advanced skills, techniques and ideas with precision and fluency. Drawing on what they know of the principles of advanced strategies and tactics or composition, they consistently apply these principles with originality, proficiency and flair in their own and others' work. . . . They reach judgements independently about how their own and others' performance could be improved, prioritising aspects for further development . . . (DfEE/QCA, 1999, p. 43)

Nature or Nurture?

Time here does not allow a full discussion of the nature–nurture argument, which is a complicated and controversial subject (e.g., Harris, 1998; Ceci and Williams, 1999). The notion of inherited talent is an appealing and commonsense explanation of what underlies skill in sport. In reviewing the literature, Ericson (1993) concluded that the role of nurture in the development of exceptional performance has repeatedly been delegated to a subsidiary place in explanation of expertise, even though the evidence for genetic factors is somewhat equivocal. Similarly, Howe and colleagues (1998, p. 2) concluded that 'differences in early experiences, preferences, opportunities, habits, training and practice are the real determinants of excellence'. In perhaps the most comprehensive study of talent development (that included development of athletic/psychomotor ability), Bloom (1985) found that no matter how much initial ability individuals had, they still had to go through years of education and training to fulfil their goal. However, Freeman (1998) found considerable evidence that small biological differences do exist between talented children and other children, suggesting that teaching, though very important, can only take a pupil on to a personal limit. In their review of musical talent, Howe and colleagues (1998) suggest five properties of talent:

1. It originates in genetically transmitted structures and hence is at least partly innate.
2. Its full effects may not be evident at an early stage but there will be some advance indications, allowing trained people to identify the presence of talent before exceptional standards of mature performance have been demonstrated.
3. These early indications of talent provide a basis for predicting who is likely to excel.
4. Only a minority are talented; if all children were talented, then there would be no way to predict or explain differential success.
5. Talents are relatively domain-specific.

Characteristics of Talented Pupils

Talented pupils, above all else, are young people with individual characteristics, distinct personality traits and strengths and weaknesses like everyone else. They ought *not* to be treated as a homogeneous group as the characteristics of talented children are extremely varied. Indeed, it would be foolish to imagine there is a typical talented pupil; only a quick glance at pupils within a physical education class tells us this is so. Talented children are usually emotionally stable, healthy and accepted by peers (Glass *et al.*, 1982; Freeman, 1998). This seems to be particularly the case where their ability expresses itself in a highly valued domain like physical competence. In his classic study of social status of teenagers, Coleman (1961) found that sporting prowess was the major factor affecting popularity of boys during adolescence. More recently, research by Weiss and Duncan (1992) has supported Coleman's findings, whilst extending their applications to all ages of children and both sexes. Children, it seems, gain acceptance by being perceived as 'good' at activities that are prized by their peers and society in general. However, for talented young performers who are much more advanced in skill and understanding than their contemporaries, there can be tension and conflict since they consistently dominate the games they play (Webb, 1993).

Talented children are usually hungry to learn (Kaplan, 1996); they can be obsessive about achieving a goal and desiring perfection to the point of anxiety. Other characteristics that talented children *may* demonstrate are:

- Alertness and vibrancy
- Energy and drive
- Persistence
- Perceptiveness
- Heightened curiosity
- The ability to reason and generalize beyond their years
- Eagerness to question and assume leadership roles (e.g., in play activities).

(Based on Renzulli, 1995; Freeman, 1998; Van Tassel-Baska 1994.)

Identification of Talented Children

We do not have so many (talented) children that we can afford to . . . make it difficult for them to emerge. (Rowlands, 1974, p. 25)

As all children have the right to 'effective learning opportunities' which 'respond to pupils' diverse learning needs' (DfEE/QCA, 1999, p. 30), teachers will need accurate assessment and recording procedures on which to base their decisions (see Chapter 5). This is a worrying aspect for talented pupils as research into teachers' assessment skills demonstrates this is often a weak area (OfSTED, 2001).

At first it would seem that teachers should not have a problem in identifying talented pupils, since they should naturally stand out from their peers. Sadly, this is not always the case as a number of factors make identification problematic. Certainly the nature of the services available to the school, such as teacher expertise and resources, and advisory support will help determine the identification procedure. Moreover, teachers may have to judge a pupil's future capability from current measurable achievement, as potential cannot be directly measured. This recognition of potential for high-level performance is a vital factor for physical education teachers who will need to identify early ('raw') talent; spotting a flash of inspiration during a critical incident may be the briefest, yet most crucial of opportunities a teacher may get (Marjoran, 1988).

Some children enter school almost a year older (more experienced) than their peers and this maturity can have a residual effect throughout secondary school. In physical education particularly, the effects of maturation can significantly affect a pupil's level of performance (Malina and Bouchard, 1991). Children who experience a stage of early and rapid growth can dominate physical education, and appear to be more talented than their less mature, but potentially more able contemporaries. This seems to be supported by research on junior distance athletes which found that only a very small percentage of successful junior distance runners went on to be senior champions (Brown, 1992).

The research into birth dates and sporting achievement in football certainly points to some interesting evidence as to how talent is being identified. Over half of the young footballers selected for the FA's Centre of Excellence were born in the first quarter of the year after the cut-off date and similar figures have been produced for other sports (e.g., Helsen *et al.*, 2000). In an interesting study in Belgium, the football authorities changed the birth date cut-off point for year group selection with dramatic effects. When the cut-off point was switched from 1 August to 1 January a major shift occurred in boys identified for the national squad. Whereas formerly August-to-October birthdays dominated the squad, the change to January drastically reduced this group, and the number of players born in January to March came to dominate. Helsen and colleagues (2000) concluded that coaches appeared to prioritize early maturation and physical precocity. They also found that there was increased risk of children born late in the selection year dropping out.

There are some clear lessons for physical education:

- In terms of equality of opportunity, teachers must ensure they are not simply associating the more physically mature pupils with high ability. Skill or potential skill and tactical understanding are better measures. Teachers must ensure their assessment methods allow for maturation levels and all pupils are given a fair opportunity to work at the highest level.
- Curriculum activities and pupil grouping must be designed to allow for pupils who may be a full year apart in maturation level.
- Teachers must consider the psychological and physical impact for less mature pupils competing against physically more mature

peers in the same year group. As Helsen and colleagues (2000, p. 730) point out, 'confidence and commitment . . . might be affected by having to compete against physically more advanced children'. Contact sports such as rugby may be particularly problematic and require careful attention by the teacher.

- In extra-curricular activities consider using maturational squads rather than year groups.
- Teachers must be alive to the development of the late bloomer.

Assessment is also made difficult because talented pupils can have a confused attitude towards their ability, and can disguise their talent, not wishing to stand out and receive negative appraisals from other pupils. This is less likely to be a problem for boys in many physical education activities where excellence in sport tends to bring status (Bailey, 1999b). However, in activities that are considered feminine (e.g., dance) boys may be reluctant to demonstrate high ability owing to peer pressure. For girls, the notion of being talented at physical education may be especially difficult as sport has tradition-ally been seen as a male pursuit. Boys often react in a hostile manner to a talented girl, especially if she is seen as a threat to their dominance (Macfadyen, 1999). For the girl, it may be a more appealing option not to develop her full potential than to risk abusive name-calling. Perhaps not coincidentally, research suggests that although both boys and girls learn to suppress their talent in order not to stand out, girls do so more prevalently (Freeman, 1998).

Evidence suggests accuracy in predicting achievement improves as children become older. This is partly because 'many (talented) children will not spontaneously show their gifts. Only after exposure to training do many children learn the skills easily, show rapid advancement, and continue to become more and more interested in their special areas' (Kaplan, 1996, p. 429). Furthermore, since chil-dren can have high ability and a strong intrinsic motivation in one specific field, subject-specific identification is usually most reliable (Freeman, 1998). This may explain why some pupils who show little or no aptitude for other academic areas only shine in physical education. Imagine a junior Paul Gascoigne or David Beckham, who may sometimes be perceived as lacking in intelligence (perhaps because of a lack of language development), but who, on a football pitch, can scan a fast-moving, ever-changing series of events, whilst analysing defensive weaknesses to pick out, in a fraction of a second, a defence splitting pass from the many options available. In such circumstances, the word talented seems less out of place. It is possible that pupils require several aspects of intelligence (e.g., analytical, creative, spatial, practical) to exhibit such high level 'game intelligence' which therefore needs to be recognized as an exceptional talent that requires special treatment.

Research on motor behaviour by Schmidt (1983) and Baba (1993), for example, suggests that an individual's performance on one motor task cannot predict performance on another, so teachers must remain alive to the possibility of a pupil excelling in an area not previously covered in the curriculum. This means that physical educators will have to be on their guard against stereotyping and have an important role in unearthing and nurturing talented children. In physical education, reliance is placed on teacher assessment to identify the most able pupils. Research by Howe and colleagues (1998) suggests that trained people can identify advance indicators of the presence of talent before an exceptional standard is reached. However, a problem for the physical education profession is whether teachers are actually sufficiently knowledgeable across the range of activities to accurately identify the most able.

Despite guidance on identification improving, a significant problem remains since teachers are inevitably caught up in a relationship with their pupils and can have their judgements biased by personal and cultural factors. Sharp and Green (1975) alert us to the possibility that certain pupils may not be considered 'able' because they cannot break through the teacher's 'reified typification' of what constitutes an able pupil. It may be no coincidence then that more boys are identified as 'able' compared to girls, perhaps because they fit stereotyped images of a talented pupil, whereas traditional images of girls' femininity do not sit comfortably with those of being talented. The dominant masculine hegemony of physical education presents the subject with a particularly acute problem in identifying able girls, except in sports perceived as feminine (e.g., dance; gym). Kaplan (1996) has estimated that 2–5 per cent of all children with disabilities are gifted or talented, and teachers must be careful not to focus solely on pupils' apparent disabilities and ignore their strengths. It would be unfortunate to miss a child's unique ability in physical education because too much emphasis was placed on remediating the disability or the pupil was not given the opportunity to excel.

Teachers' judgements, however, can be pivotal. Creativity, for example, is notoriously difficult to measure: 'sometimes . . . the unorthodox response can only be truly appreciated by the expert' (Marjoran, 1988, p. 29). The difficulty is that teachers tend not to be very reliable sources of identification (Freeman, 1998), although this ability can improve with training (Richert, 1991). Where they are kept manageable, check lists can act as useful pointers and stimulate teachers to consider identification issues more closely. Perhaps their best use is 'in planning and providing approaches and stimuli required to challenge able pupils' (Marjoran, 1988, p. 37). In effect, the National Curriculum End of Key Stage Levels act as check lists for teachers. Pupils who work significantly beyond the expected level may therefore be considered talented, which can act as the stimulus to ensure more challenging work is fed into their programme. The advantage of using these levels is that teachers can build up a comprehensive pupil profile over time to check against the criteria, whilst remaining within the National Curriculum framework.

Of course, checklists are not without problems: the criteria used still relies on the question setter's background so can be open to cultural bias, and actually putting a checklist together can be difficult. Research by HMI (1992) found that where schools used checklists, only a few made use of sufficiently specific criteria. Furthermore, there remains a danger of over-reliance: the child can be lost within the labels, and potentially able children who do not fit can be missed. Checklists can construe ability too simply: pupils either have a lot, some or a little of it. Physical ability is a diverse construct that does not follow this pattern. Helsen and colleagues (2000) have pointed out that research makes it difficult to support the notion that sport expertise can be predicted on the basis of any specific measure of talent.

Perhaps the key point is that assessment needs to be continuous, systematic and multi-dimensional as children's development fluctuates: regular assessment means provision can be fine tuned and more effectively directed. A broad assessment procedure, involving both subjective and objective measures, will help to moderate out biases since the strengths of one technique can balance out the weaknesses of another. This is important as failure to resolve issues of validity will lead to meaningless assessment packages.

Richert (1991) has produced a useful set of standards that he believes all procedures for identifying talented pupils should meet so that they are fair and equitable:

- Advocacy: the identification process should be designed so that it will be in the best interests of all pupils.
- Defensibility: the procedures should be based upon research in the area of education for talented children.

- Equity: the identification procedure should not overlook minority pupils or pupils with disabilities who often fail to gain acceptance into such programmes.
- Pluralism: the definition of talented should be broad enough to identify many areas.
- Comprehensiveness: as many talented pupils should be identified and served as possible.
- Pragmatism: whenever possible, procedures should allow for modification and use a number of different sources of information.

Provision for Talented Pupils in Physical Education

It is a myth that talented children achieve just because they are talented. There is overwhelming evidence of the necessity for support and guidance for talented children (e.g., Freeman, 1998; Young and Tyre, 1992; OfSTED 1995). Relevant studies support the need for differentiated strategies as the needs of a talented pupil are often atypical (Van Tassel-Baska, 1994). The statutory inclusion statement within the National Curriculum (DfEE/QCA, 1999) strongly encourages teachers to set suitable learning challenges which includes identification of the needs of the more able:

> For pupils whose attainments significantly exceed the expected level of attainment ... teachers will need to plan suitably challenging work. As well as drawing on materials from later key stages or higher levels of study, teachers may plan further differentiation by extending the breadth and depth of study ... or by planning work which draws on the content of different subjects. (DfEE/QCA, 1999, p. 29)

Traditionally, there have been four main strategies to differentiate learning for the very able: acceleration, pupil grouping, enrichment and extension, the latter two being clearly laid out in the National Curriculum. Acceleration can save a gifted pupil a year of unnecessary time in school as it usually involves 'grade skipping': moving a pupil up a year group in order to present work more in line with their understanding.

It is most relevant to a pupil demonstrating high ability *across the curriculum* and continually outstripping peers. It has been found to be effective (Van Tassel-Baska, 1994) but a significant problem lies in its inflexibility since a pupil may excel in physical education and require advanced work, but for other subjects jumping a year ahead may be completely inappropriate. A sensible compromise is 'partial acceleration' where a pupil is accelerated only in physical education since the use of 'significant others' can enhance learning for the talented through peer modelling (Van Tassel-Baska, 1994). However, as partial acceleration may be impractical, promotion to the next year group, to play with better, more experienced players, can be achieved through extra-curricular activities.

Since talented pupils can not only learn faster than their peers but are ready to go farther afield to explore wider areas of knowledge, acceleration alone will be insufficient. Enrichment makes special provision for a pupil through any modification to teaching that provides more challenge and more variety than regular class work affords. This means that the pupil can be appropriately educated in their regular class. Enrichment should not mean simply more of the same work, which leads only to inadequate learning opportunities and boredom. Instead, enrichment (e.g., analysis and interpretation) *replaces*, rather than supplements, the repetitive basics. For example, an able pupil could be given work on associated topics to consider. Bailey (2000a), for example, has identified a number of wide-ranging citizenship issues relevant to physical education that could make appropriate enrichment work.

A key advantage of enrichment is the flexibility to adapt to the pupil's changing needs, so that provision can remain in tune with development. Tempest (1974) found that the most able pupils could flourish in the normal classroom if they were taught in a challenging and interesting manner. The nature of enrichment means that it promotes a pupil's hidden potential too, as it encourages pupils to develop their understanding, encounter and form new ideas, and solve problems by formulating new methods. Moon and colleagues (1994) report that a directed enrichment programme helped pupils achieve considerably higher levels of attainment. In support, Torrence (1987) found sufficient evidence that creativity could be successfully taught through different types of enriched teaching.

Enrichment does need to be kept up, otherwise pupils slip back to the level of their (equally able) peers who have not had the enrichment experience (Tempest, 1974; Moon *et al.*, 1994). Van Tassel-Baska (1994) has highlighted the importance of a range of teachers with differing characteristics for the talented pupil, but this needs to be weighed up against the benefits of continuity provided by the same teacher staying with a class over an extended period. If this is not possible, the importance of passing over detailed information (e.g., through a profile on the strengths and weaknesses of the pupil) is evident.

Since there is little point in 'teaching' pupils something they already know, teachers will need to consider carefully a pupil's correct 'entry point' (difficulty level) into the curriculum by assessing them at the start of a scheme of work. This will facilitate extension: the practice of allowing children to 'skip sections' or move through the curriculum more quickly (Eyre and Marjoram, 1990). The National Curriculum allows teachers to pick work from the Key Stage above the child's current level so it is up to teachers not to be slavish to a given format, but to be flexible and adaptable within the curriculum to reward pupil progress with appropriate work. Where talented pupils have skipped sections of work, they should be thoroughly assessed to ensure they have acquired all the movement 'basics' so there is no possibility of gaps in their knowledge and they have the 'foundations' for future high level work.

Van Tassel-Baska (1994) has suggested that diagnostic assessment, followed by *individualization*, are essential strategies for use with talented pupils. Teachers can draw on similar strategies for additional or individual support to those currently utilized with pupils with learning difficulties. Individual Education Plans (IEPs), along with associated support from non-teaching assistants, can provide a structured approach to identifying and ensuring appropriate provision for talented pupils (e.g., simply utilizing more complex sport specific terminology).

Physical educators have hardly been helped by the lack of research and training given to them in this specific field and the mixed results found by Treffinger and colleagues (1996) on the success of enrichment suggests teachers will have to work hard at managing the needs of the most able. Perhaps the key point for teachers is that working with talented children requires a thorough examination of the opportunities they offer pupils (Leyden, 1990). Teachers may well be advised to ask themselves whether the scheme(s) of work planned contain the educational objectives to:

- Help learners develop proficiently *at a sufficient level of difficulty*.
- Ensure a rich and complete treatment of the topic.
- Help talented learners become creatively productive.
- Allow for a diversity that promotes self-directed learning and the enhancement of independent investigations.
- Increase the interest and motivation for the topic.

(From Van Tassel-Baska, 1994)

It is important for teachers not to be anxious or embarrassed by the superior competence of talented pupils or to put a 'ceiling' on their learning because they feel they cannot cope with pupils' levels of development (e.g., by constraining a pupil within direct teaching methods). Much more effective is likely to be the exploration of new work *in partnership* with the pupil, using the pupil's expertise as a performer and the teacher's expertise as a facilitator. The advantage of working with (older) secondary pupils is that teachers can effectively set joint goals since these pupils will know more about their learning, capabilities and requirements than primary age children. Evidence suggests that the very able are particularly 'stimulated and challenged when actively involved in their own learning' (HMI, 1993, p. 10).

Despite the benefits of direct teaching styles (Macfadyen, 2000), teachers must ensure that the 'drill' and practice activities they present are appropriate so a talented pupil's creativity is not stifled by a lack of freedom. Ill-conceived 'drill' type work can level down pupils, inhibit individualized instruction, reduce the meaningfulness of the work and prevent a rapid learner undertaking harder tasks more quickly. Research suggests that talented children have a more mature and indeed different learning style to other children (Span, 1995), and too much structure can interfere with their learning (Snow, 1989). Van Tassel-Baska (1994) has pointed out that talented pupils profit from a curriculum that allows for flexible approaches to solutions rather than tightly prescribed teaching methods. Talented pupils seem to enjoy and thrive on problem solving and open-ended tasks (Marjoran, 1988) and have been found to become frustrated if unable to ask their own questions (Leyden, 1990). Thus Marjoran (1988, p. 58) has suggested 'controlled freedom' as the way forward (e.g., pupils devise and lead warm-ups, or invent new games/practices devised to teach their peers a set objective).

Differentiation by outcome will tend to suit talented pupils as it gives them a free hand to experiment and pupils are not tied down to the teacher's (limited) expectations of the class. It is vital that talented pupils are encouraged to experiment and not to be afraid of failure so they can learn from their mistakes, formulate plans, find solutions and understand fully what they can achieve. It can be helpful for the teacher to publicly praise the talented pupil even when they fail at a difficult task, to create a climate where creativity and exploration are highly valued. Clearly, assessment methods will need to reflect such a policy. This may be particularly important in the secondary sector where pupils are often more reluctant to take risks and the pressure of the peer group to conform is so great.

Further guidance on differentiation strategies is available in Chapter 7, and applies equally here.

Pupil grouping has perplexed educators for many years. The question of whether to educate the most able pupils separately or include them in mixed-ability classes remains controversial. Often the argument is used that the most able should remain in mixed-ability classes to prevent the less able from becoming de-motivated and feeling rejected by the school system. It is also argued that the presence of the most able helps the less able, though this assertion is not proven in the research. However, in practical terms, teachers often pitch the lesson at the middle ability range in mixed ability lessons, (Freeman, 1998) which runs contrary to the need to have very high expectations and to set very high challenges for talented children. Some research has suggested that many children are seriously underestimated by their teachers (Leyden, 1990; Young and Tyre, 1992; HMI, 1993). This may be because 'many OfSTED inspections have highlighted the lack of coherent and effective school policies targeting the upper end of the continuum of children's abilities' (Koshy *et al.*, 1995, p. 29). Many teachers have not received specific training or had relevant experiences in high ability work that enables them to appreciate the capabilities of the talented. Feldhusen (1994, p. 367) is particularly scathing of mixed ability classes for the most able, claiming 'most severely limiting of all, are the efforts to provide for (talented) youth in mixed, heterogeneous classrooms'.

Many schools do now set their pupils (the grouping of pupils according to their ability in a particular subject), especially older secondary pupils. Setting is often seen as more preferable to streaming (assigning pupils to classes on the basis of an overall assessment of ability; pupils remain in their streamed class for the majority of subjects) as the latter lacks the ability to recognize pupils' different abilities in different subjects. Setting, it is claimed, reduces the ability range within the class, making teaching more efficient. Given the wide difference between attributes required for dance, gym, outdoor activities, games, swimming and athletic events, it would seem somewhat ironic for schools to set for physical education per se, and not then reset within the subject for the different activities. As a marginal subject, physical education often 'inherits' pupil grouping as a consequence of other subjects' setting. Other physical education departments have consciously decided on a mixed ability policy while others still set for physical education. Such differences in pupil grouping demonstrate the wide range of opinions that exist towards this policy.

Experience suggests that flexible grouping is recommendable for different parts of a lesson (and for different activities) and where enrichment activities utilize pupil grouping they must be carefully thought through. Considerable evidence suggests that talented pupils should be given the opportunity to work alongside similarly able peers (Kaplan, 1996; Gross, 1993), particularly when the material is complex, since working with equally able peers 'is an important component in affirming ability (that can in turn improve motivation) as well as providing a challenging milieu for the development of specific talent' (Van Tassel-Baska, 1994, p. 27). Since talented pupils have been found to be very good at modelling the behaviours of others who are succeeding (Feldhusen, 1994), the policy of 'cluster grouping' able pupils within a mixed ability lesson may be of great benefit. For example, when performing a gymnastics mirror sequence, pairing two equally able pupils together would seem to be advantageous, as they will complement each other, by pushing each other on and allowing them to perform to the best of their ability.

Teachers sometimes ask an able pupil to teach a less able peer to help bring the latter's standard up. However, teachers must also consider how this fits into the most able pupil's programme. Teaching others can be of great benefit since it provides a new perspective and challenge and such tasks can work exceptionally well as long as able pupils have been given the 'tools' to implement such a policy, and they understand their own limitations (in this new area) and those of their partner. During a striking and fielding practice, where less able pupils require an accurate feed, it would be sensible to place them with very able pupils. The former then receive a high quality delivery, and the latter have the genuine challenge of consistently sending accurate 'feeds' and fielding any inaccurate returns.

Leyden (1990) has suggested that the flexibility required for teaching talented pupils may be beyond the scope of the normal class. For such reasons special schools for children with special attributes, such as sporting ability, do seem to have a place in the education system:

> Some gifts . . . notably . . . the performing arts do seem to call for special full-time education so that children can immerse themselves more deeply than in a normal school – and so move on more quickly within their discipline. (Freeman, 1998, p. 43)

Even where specialist schools are not available, Education Authorities can pool talented teachers to support a Physical Education Academy where a group of talented pupils from various schools meet together at regular intervals with the teacher most suited to support them.

Local schools can also co-operate to provide a variety of after-school advanced sports clubs (as well as those for the less talented enthusiasts). Since the teacher of physical education should facilitate the highest achievement a pupil can attain, many pupils will need to be encouraged to take their talent further afield. The growing importance of partnerships between schools and national governing bodies and other sports institutions means the teacher's bridging role (finding pathways for talented pupils) will be a vital one. Since opportunity (e.g., availability of facilities) can have an effect on determining the fulfilment of talent, as little as possible should be left to chance.

True partnerships between schools and parents/carers are also invaluable, as the wider support of the family is absolutely critical if pupils are to reach the highest levels (Freeman, 1998; Gross, 1993; Tannenbaum, 1983). Information sharing, not just information giving, is the key principle towards more fruitful communication.

In order to plan effective work for talented pupils, physical education departments must understand the special needs of the population involved. Presented below is a summary for teaching talented pupils in physical education:

- New knowledge should not be presented in isolation, but incorporated within the overall context of physical education so learning experiences have continuity.
- Facilitate the learning of high level generic movement skills and analysis so pupils can expand on material for themselves at any point in and out of lessons.
- Provide opportunities for divergent production of knowledge (e.g., allow pupils to devise and solve tactical conundrums from a loose framework).
- Encourage pupils to follow their interests by providing greater exposure to new areas of learning outside the curriculum and school structure.
- Help pupils link up their knowledge and understanding to other curriculum areas and see how physical education interrelates to other bodies of knowledge (e.g., the role of dance to transmit culture).
- Set high goals (even to a professional standard where appropriate) that demand imaginative experimentation (e.g., gymnastics floor work, dance choreography). Where appropriate, generate real audiences and outlets for pupil performances.
- Create advanced classes that allow talented pupils to come together socially (to prevent any feelings of being 'different')

and which provide for their special needs by accelerating the pace and depth of the physical education programme.

- Appoint a sports mentor from the community to provide ongoing individual talent development. It may be particularly important to provide girls with a female role model.

Conclusions

As provision for talented pupils will be a long-term issue and will have to be written down and widely communicated, it will need to be a whole department issue. However, it may be wise to delegate the co-ordination and development of talent to one particular staff member whose responsibility will be to provide information and support colleagues. Teachers' capacities to spot the talented child should not be underestimated; many teachers have worked extremely hard to develop their own techniques and resources to cope with these pupils. The key would seem to be to draw together the good practice currently being used, and to disseminate this excellence to help teachers educate their talented youngsters.

Talented children are best viewed as normal children with exceptional aptitudes. Teachers can make a considerable difference to whether young people fulfil their potential through encouragement, inspiration and providing the right opportunities. Since identifying a talented pupil is so complex, it is likely many very able pupils will not be picked out. Research by Bloom (1985) found that the majority of people who had reached the top in sport had not been regarded as child prodigies, and only 10 per cent had progressed far enough by aged 12 to make any prediction about their future ascendancy to the top. Even within the narrow concerns of very able pupils, therefore, it seems sensible to keep the maximum number of young people as possible involved in physical activity, for the greatest possible length of time.

Every pupil deserves to be taught to the level of which they are capable at that moment in time. Talented children's learning can and should be enhanced by well-planned and skilfully executed teaching, which will require a combination of methods since no one particular system can claim to be the final answer to a pupil's needs. If we want our most talented pupils to go on to be the next generation of leaders of physical education and sport, these pupils will need to develop certain skills on top of their physical precocity: creative excellence, autonomy, independent thinking, and self-actualization. If this is to happen, the way talented pupils are taught as well as what they are taught will require careful analysis.

CHAPTER 9

Safe Learning in Physical Education

*Safety . . . does not consist merely of the absence of accidents but a
positive mental and physical security which comes from the
knowledge that all the teacher's responsibilities have been
recognised and met.*
(O'Connor, 1987, p. 25)

Introduction

The concept of safety should be a priority throughout the planning
and delivery of physical education lessons. This is because of all the
curricula subjects, physical education probably has the greatest
potential for creating situations where accidents resulting in bodily
injury can occur. During the course of physical education lessons
pupils are expected to move their bodies vigorously, run and change
direction at high speed, jump over apparatus, strike with imple-
ments, make use of limited space, work in areas that may not have
been constantly monitored and are open to the elements, operate
in and by deep water and much more. So it is a responsibility of
all those working in physical education to contribute to the provision of a strong safety culture that allows pupils to undertake
a range of exciting and challenging activities without coming to
harm.

The purpose of this chapter is to explain how teachers can reduce
the chance of pupils being physically damaged in the course of
physical education by considering the application of some of the key
safety principles. The first section examines teachers' duty of care.
This is followed by a consideration of the contribution teachers need
to make to risk assessment and their role in reducing the level of
danger, and a discussion of a selection of other factors that can have
a significant bearing on the level of risk of accident in the physical

education lesson. Finally, the chapter considers the importance of pupils' awareness of safety issues.

Duty of Care

Whilst most physical education teachers would probably consider the provision of a safe environment to be part of their normal professional functions (Clay, 1997), it has to be remembered that teachers and schools have a significant responsibility for safety which is underpinned by law. Teachers in the United Kingdom are considered to be *in loco parentis*, and this responsibility includes a duty of care for the safety of the pupils in their charge. The level of care to be taken by those in physical education was at one time based on what might be expected of a reasonably prudent parent. However, the British Association of Advisers and Lecturers in Physical Education (BAALPE, 1995, p. 23) has noted that

> Over the years it has been established through the courts that a school teacher should be expected to know a good deal more about the propensities of children than might a prudent parent. Add to this that some aspects of physical education have a high level of risk and required awareness and a higher duty of care is now expected of physical education teachers.

In order to provide this higher duty of care it would seem essential that those teaching physical education have appropriate training, qualifications and experience for the activities with which they are involved, and to be able to apply their knowledge of the changing structure and nature of the growing child to assist in safeguarding the well-being of pupils in their charge.

Qualifications

In order to deliver a higher duty of care over the full range of curriculum physical education, teachers need to be knowledgeable about the full range of activities taught, and be able to plan, present and evaluate lessons effectively. Given the time restrictions with respect to physical education within some Initial Teacher Training courses (Warburton, 1999), it could be supposed, that not all newly qualified teachers will feel completely confident safely conducting lessons over the whole range of activities. Even when deemed qualified, teachers should not attempt to teach an activity or skill above their present level of competence.

Teachers without the necessary expertise can upgrade their qualifications in a variety of ways. In-service courses may be made available through local, national and academic providers and many governing bodies of sport have designed courses for teachers. In addition to physical education qualifications, it is advisable for those teaching physical education to have at least basic first aid training, whilst a thorough knowledge of the school's accident and emergency arrangements is essential.

Knowledge about Young People

Knowledge of children's development is an important factor in the appropriate application of physical education in the secondary school. Teachers need to be aware of safe exercises for young people and the safety implications of pupils' individual differences. Teachers will have to be alert to the implications of classmates, who are at very different stages of maturation, working together. In gymnastics, for example, it may be worth matching pupils of equal height or weight to support each other.

As children grow and their bodies change shape, differences in proportions can have a significant effect on the performance of skills. Balance, dexterity, co-ordination and timing of actions can all suffer as some children appear temporarily awkward and suddenly unable to move with the control they exhibited previously. It will be important for teachers to understand and show sensitivity to these changes. For example, the teacher should not necessarily expect pupils to perform certain gymnastic moves in the upper school because they were able to do them in the previous Key Stage.

Safety for with Pupils with Special Needs

Familiarity with a school's policy on pupils with special needs is essential to maintaining a safe environment in physical education. Pupils' medical conditions (e.g., asthma, diabetes and arthritis) can affect practice and teachers will need to be sensitive to individual differences. Unless specifically forbidden, all pupils should actively participate in lessons, albeit with some precautions when required. For example, a pupil with epilepsy, who may be subject to 'absences', can readily participate in low-level gymnastics but will be ill-advised to climb up high due to their potential loss of consciousness.

Safely integrating pupils' individual needs into physical education can present a real challenge to teachers. The teacher will usually need to consider a number of issues in this regard:

- How can the chosen physical activity be safely adapted/modified to best meet the individual's needs?

- What are the implications of the identified impairment for the pupil, teacher and other class members?
- Will extra support be required, and if so how can it be most effectively employed?
- For pupils with a sensory impairment, what communication issues need to be addressed to ensure the pupil remains safe?

(Based on Perkins, 1997)

Teacher as Role Model

The quality of teachers' leadership is a vital principle of safety as teachers can set good examples to pupils at a time when role models are very important. Personal presentation and clothing can set the right example and teachers can set out through their words and actions the importance of safety in physical education. As the DES (1980, p. 1) have rightly suggested, 'the prevention of accidents largely depends on the skill, knowledge and example of the teacher'. It is therefore incumbent on the physical educator to set the appropriate tone or atmosphere for a given activity. In activities such as athletic throwing events or certain gymnastic activities, the teacher's persona will have to be calm and serious to stress that no nonsense will be tolerated.

Welch (1978, p. ix) has suggested that 'accidents are part of the constant trial and error process of living' and to some extent this is paralleled in physical education. Teachers will therefore need the ability to anticipate, think quickly and intervene appropriately to prevent minor accidents resulting from pupil explorations becoming serious. This means monitoring the whole class all the time.

Risk Assessment

The identification and management of risk is an essential part of every teacher's duty, and helps to ensure that even some of the most challenging activities can be attempted by pupils without damage. The trick, of course, is to reduce the level of danger by a series of strategies and procedures, yet still retain those elements an activity can provide, such as a sense of adventure, mastery of a task, expenditure of effort, challenge, and individual expression, which can be so rewarding.

Risk assessment consists of a set of procedures through which hazards and those who may be harmed by them can be identified, and then control measures devised to prevent the possibility of accidents occurring from the foreseen dangers: 'Risk assessment emphasises the estimation and quantification of risk in order to determine acceptable levels of risk and safety; in other words to balance the risks of an . . . activity against its . . . benefits' (Cutter, 1993, p. 2). Effective risk assessment should mean that the only risks pupils assume are those that are an inherent part of the activity. The National Coaching Foundation (1986) defines inherent risks as *the risks left over* when everything possible has been done to make an activity as safe as possible.

The ways in which identified risks are managed need to be recorded. BAALPE (1995, p. 44) advises that the process of risk assessment 'should form an integral part of schemes of work and lesson planning'. The same authority also states that risk assessment should be applied when foreseeable risks or hazards may occur. Due to the nature of the subject, it would seem sensible to appraise most activities in the physical education curriculum, whilst recognizing that some require more attention than others. Thus, activities can be placed on a continuum according to the perceived level of risk they exhibit (Kelly, 1997): most dance activities may be placed at the lower end of the continuum, and certain gymnastics or outdoor pursuits at a higher point.

As a result of a risk-assessment exercise it may be concluded that a particular activity is potentially too hazardous for inclusion in the school's physical education programme, at least in some forms. Some activities and equipment are actually prohibited by some Education Authorities. At a local level it may be necessary, following a risk assessment, to preclude an activity from the physical education programme because it is not possible, given prevailing conditions, to reduce identified risks to a reasonable level. Banning netball because the surface of the only playing area becomes too uneven or slippery to move about without fear of accident illustrates the point.

Such is the breadth of the physical education curriculum that even specialists may not have in-depth knowledge of all the activities being undertaken in their school. In such cases it would be wise to call for advice when required.

Negligence

In recent years, a number of writers have noted the mounting legislation and growing litigation in physical education (Eve, 1997; Harrison and Watkins, 1996), which has meant more serious accidents are often subject to an enquiry. Kelly (1997) notes that current law considers the environment, supervision and instruction as the three key areas of an investigation. Being found to be negligent in an incident is probably a teacher's greatest anxiety. However, by showing they have taken reasonable precautions and have followed standard practice (e.g., can be seen to have carried out the relevant safety rules and followed the accident procedure after an accident) physical educators can significantly reduce the risk of litigation.

Other Factors Affecting Safety in Physical Education

Research suggests a safe and orderly environment is usually paramount for learning to take place (Hill and Hill, 1994). Noticing and dealing appropriately with hazards is an ongoing responsibility for those teaching physical education and they may be assisted in their endeavours by considering the following factors. It should be noted, however, that the following points do not make up an exhaustive list. Teachers should refer for detailed guidelines to definitive texts on safety (e.g., BAALPE, 1999a).

Premises

While each physical education activity will have its own distinctive risks, there are generic potential hazards arising from the nature of facilities in which lessons take place. Thus, for activities that take place indoors special attention must be paid to the design and construction of the accommodation, the floor surface and obstructions, while outdoors the playing surface and general environment need to be examined and any necessary precautionary procedures implemented.

A. Indoor facilities

i) Design and construction of the accommodation
Many physical education lessons will not be carried out in purpose-built rooms. Sometimes, for example, lessons take place in generic school halls, and teachers conducting lessons in such areas should be on the look out for dangerous features. These might include doors that open inward, protruding handles, radiators and low-level unprotected glazed areas. The space adjacent to these hazards must be cordoned-off in an obvious way and viewed as a 'no go' zone. Activities that include running and other fast movement must be organized in such a way that children could not possibly come into contact with the dangers, or not be included in the programme.

ii) Floor surface
Teachers should always be alert to situations that can change conditions. Dirt brought in on outdoor shoes, spilt drinks, and leaks, can

all turn a normally safe floor into one with dangerous slippery patches. Inspection of the floor area should take place before the start of the lesson and arrangements should be in place for dirty floors to be swept and spillages mopped up as soon as they are discovered.

iii) Obstructions

Teachers must be aware of furniture, a piano or other equipment that may intrude into a multi-purpose working area. Co-operation and negotiation with other teachers and supervisory staff is the key to ensuring as much space for safe movement as possible. Temporarily redundant items should always be stored in the same designated space and in such a way that sharp corners do not stick out. The selection of appropriate activities, good organization of the space available and sufficient margin between activity areas and storage areas should help avoid collisions between pupils and furniture.

B) Outdoor facilities

i) The playing surface

Poorly maintained surfaces which are pitted, bumpy or covered with loose material are likely to be unsafe for many physical activities, especially those involving moving balls, running and quick changes of direction. Teachers should remember that certain weather conditions can turn normally safe playing surfaces into unacceptable ones. Frost, rain and dew can all make some surfaces unsuitable for use as can occasional car parking on the hard playing area that can result in the deposit of oil patches. It is important, therefore, that the playing surface should be inspected before all lessons. Some areas that are not easily scanned and are vulnerable to outside abuse should be thoroughly checked for dangers. Pupils may be involved in a sweep search of the area so long as they can be relied upon not to touch or pick up any dangerous objects they might come across. Children should be instructed to draw the teachers' attention to any offending items found and these can be removed with the right amount of care.

ii) General environment

Appraisal, similar to that of indoor premises, is required before each physical education lesson held outdoors: for example, the state of boundary fences and the position of activity spaces in relation to them will need consideration. Additionally, the teacher must remain vigilant throughout the lesson as conditions may change: for example, an orienteering course can become unsafe because of the entry of a delivery vehicle to the school grounds.

C) Swimming pools

Public swimming pools have well-established safety regulations that are normally strictly enforced by trained staff. Teachers should be aware of the regulations, and support the on-site professionals. When a school's own pool or a private pool is utilized, similarly strict safety regulations should be adhered to, including staff qualifications and staff:pupil ratios.

Equipment

Two main kinds of physical education equipment can usually be found in secondary schools: gymnastic equipment and portable equipment.

i) Gymnastic equipment

This can be both fixed and portable. Although anchored to a wall or ceiling, fixed apparatus (ropes, ladders, rings) often move in and out on trackways or is hinged and has to be set up manually to form a climbing frame. Portable gymnastic equipment includes pieces such as bar boxes, nesting tables, balance bars, and benches, some of which have to be assembled before use. Special consideration has to be given to proper methods of lifting and carrying portable apparatus and to the neat and safe storage of this kind of apparatus. Dangerous situations can quickly arise from poor handling of equipment or untidiness.

When, as is often the case, pupils are involved in setting out gymnastic equipment, a three-stage checking protocol should be completed by the teacher before any one moves on to any piece. Stage one involves the teacher checking that the equipment has been correctly positioned and that each piece is in sufficient space to allow movements on to, from, through and over it without fear of pupils bumping into walls or other obstructions or interfering with other activities. In the second stage of the checking process the teacher should ensure that the apparatus is stable, has been properly assembled and should note particularly that any locking pins/fixing bolts implicated in the assembly process are securely engaged. The third stage of the inspection routine should concentrate on the condition of the equipment. Occurrences such as accidental collisions or vandalism could cause splinters to be present in wooden beams or perhaps vibration might cause screws or bolts to work loose. Should any problems be discovered, the apparatus should be taken out of use immediately. All those teaching physical education should feel secure in the knowledge that the apparatus they are using is inspected on a regular basis by professional engineers according to the manufacturers' recommendations.

ii) Portable equipment
Bats, hockey sticks, rackets and goal/net posts are examples of the type of equipment that might be found in secondary schools. They may seem innocuous enough stacked in the store cupboard, but can constitute a hazard and may bring harm to the user, or those in the vicinity, if they are not of a suitable size and weight, or kept in good condition. Worn or soiled handles that can cause a performer's grip to slip can turn a striking implement into a missile.

Clothing and Jewellery
Children heat up and cool down relatively quickly compared to adults and therefore can suffer from heat stress in too warm an environment or from hypothermia when it is too cold. For these reasons children must be properly protected in extremes of temperature (e.g., on a visit to an under-heated swimming pool on a warm day, or on a playing field subjected to a bitingly cold wind). In hot conditions pupils should wear loose, lightweight clothing and where necessary be protected from the sun's rays with long-sleeved vests and hats, with parts of the skin still exposed treated with a high-factor sun cream. Conversely when it is cold they should wear sufficient layers to keep out the chill: a shivering pupil is less likely to be alert to potentially dangerous situations, and, of course, less motivated to learn. Shoes worn in physical education lessons should be flexible and have flat soles resistant to slip on the surface being used. For gym and dance, bare feet is often most appropriate. Young people should not sacrifice suitability for fashion, which can put an enormous pressure on them. For example, laces should always be tied up rather than simply tucked in.

There are very few jewellery-related accidents in schools because usually there are already procedures in place to prevent them. It is important that all teachers of physical education ensure that compliance with these procedures, which normally require removal of ornamental jewellery and other personal effects before the start of the physical education lesson remain standard practice. The exceptions are where jewellery is worn for cultural reasons. In such situations, cases should be dealt with sensitively, on an individual basis. Young people and their parents are often more receptive to the argument of removing jewellery once the consequences of an accident have been explained. Where jewellery has to be kept on, careful thought needs to be given to how the adornments can be adequately covered (e.g., surgical tape/wristbands).

Educating Pupils

It is clear that the teacher plays an essential role in producing a safe and secure physical education environment in which pupils can learn. Teachers may be wise to work to a general set of rules in all their lessons to provide pupils with an established framework of behaviour and procedure. Younger secondary-aged pupils, in particular, will need tight control, as in their enthusiasm for activity they can get carried away. At certain times, teachers will need to instruct pupils when and where to move, so everyone remains safe.

Pupils should not begin their tasks on the apparatus until the safety checks have been completed by the teacher. They will need to be taught this restraint and constantly reminded of the protocol as the equipment is likely to prove a great attraction. In the further interests of safety, pupils will also have to be taught that only an appropriate number of people can be allowed on each piece of equipment at any one time.

Teachers will need to find a balance between instructing pupils on exactly what to do, and helping them to increase their own understanding and awareness of safety. Teachers who over-regulate and simply continue to tell pupils what to do can produce pupils unable to act on their own initiative which can lead to a genuine failure to know what the rules are, and even reaction against them (Welch, 1978). Older children may be resentful of too much teacher intervention as they learn to come to terms with their own ability and the amount of risk they can safely take. Accidents are less likely to occur if learners understand what causes them, and if they are allowed to take responsibility for their actions (see Chapters 2 and 4). The Council of Europe (cited Boucher, 1977, p. 139) suggests that 'training of the child at all ages in active participation in safety behaviour is essential'. This is recognized in the National Curriculum for Physical Education (DfEE/QCA, 1999) which includes specific reference to health and safety principles that pupils should be taught (e.g., 'to recognize hazards' and 'to manage their environment', p. 39). This will be a staged process as children mature into young adults, able to take on increasingly complex safety roles.

Schools may be advised to make explicit in policy documentation how pupils' responsibility for their own and others' safety will be developed year on year. For example, Benn and Benn (1992, p. 97) suggest 'a good school policy will phase in the demands of handling apparatus alongside the development of other areas of learning in gymnastics'.

Conclusion

Safety in physical education is the teacher's first priority and should never be compromised. This chapter has suggested that safe practice underpins good practice and that safety considerations should be a natural starting point for each lesson. Accident prevention is multi-faceted but can be effectively managed through common sense and responsible risk assessment.

Anxiety about teaching physical education can become a real drain on the teacher's energy, and detract from pupil learning. The best way forward would seem to be to plan a framework that can cope with foreseen eventualities and to use appropriate regulations to guide the implementation of sound curricular physical education.

CHAPTER 10

Leadership in Physical Education

Introduction

As this book demonstrates, effective provision of physical education in secondary schools is dependent on a multitude of factors such as first-class teaching, high pupil expectations, effective curriculum organization and planning, sound systems of assessment, and the continuing professional development of staff. Heads of department have a key job, as few have a greater potential for influencing the quality of physical education that young people receive: they are close to the teaching and learning process; their position provides the opportunity to motivate staff and maximize their different skills; they lead policy decisions; they improve standards in performance; they offer advice; and they make meetings relevant and valuable. Thus, achieving the conditions that facilitate high quality provision is a critical and demanding task.

Management is a distinct type of work: the good physical education teacher does not automatically make a good manager. While technical know-how is important, management makes extra demands, as it concerns the work of people and the effectiveness of and accountability for end-results (Torkildsen, 1996). In order to effectively manage a school's resources, services and facilities, heads of department need to understand the concept of management and the skills and techniques of leadership. For many teachers, learning the leader's role on the job will be the best way to appreciate what is required, as the opportunity to practise is probably the most important factor (Keay, 1996). However, the job is sometimes made more difficult because a preparatory phase of training is often missed in schools. Thus, when a teacher first takes on a managerial role, experience of possible management styles is usually limited (Dean, 1985), and it can be difficult to assess and come to terms with the power invested in the managerial position. Some teachers may over-estimate what the role allows them to do, causing friction and resentment. Conversely, other teachers may under-estimate the effects of their new-found position.

This chapter will provide the reader with a set of ideas and principles from which to work, and help teachers consider their strengths and weaknesses that, inevitably, will shape their leadership style. For the more experienced leader, the chapter is an opportunity to enhance one's capability and, perhaps more importantly, the capabilities of departmental colleagues. It is an invitation to consider the present state of leadership knowledge and engage in serious reflection. Lastly, as every teacher has to think and act like a manager, it is hoped that this chapter will be useful for all teachers who want to improve the way they work. Indeed, Bucher and Thaxton (1981) remind us of the necessity for new leaders to emerge to continue progress; they suggest new teachers almost have an obligation to assume the reins of leadership.

Leadership or Management?

Is a head of department a leader or manager? Historically, educationalists have been wary of a manager tag because of its connotations of business/industry and of 'production'. Whilst schools are unique and complex entities, in some ways they are not very different from other organizations, since a school is a collection of 'individuals brought together for a purpose . . . subject to all the problems, limitations, and excitements that are inherent in getting people to work together, whatever they do' (Handy and Aitkin, 1986, p. 35). Whilst the context is specific, many generic management skills are relevant to education and the principles upon which they are based remain constant since managing means getting things done through other people (Dean, 1985). Handy and Aitkin (1986, p. 34) actually suggest that the different context of education is not a barrier, because 'to compare yourself with others is often the best way to begin to understand yourself'.

The difference between leadership and management has often

been blurred, since the terms are often used interchangeably. Dean (1985, p. 2) has stated:

> Good management involves working with people and resources as they are and helping them to work together to achieve agreed ends. The skilled manager looks for ways in which the interest and abilities of each individual can contribute and tries to create an organisation and a climate in which this can happen.

Whilst Eastwood and Buswell (1987, p. 36) describe the function of leadership as:

> Defining objectives, planning, communicating, delegating, supporting and controlling; doing, observing, discussing, evaluating and doing it again; fulfilling the task, building and maintaining the group and developing the individual.

Leadership and management are inextricably linked, though Dean (1985, p. 19) suggests that analysing the tasks of leadership and management can make them appear separate: 'a collection of processes taking place in the same context. In practice it isn't like that. The pieces of the puzzle are part of the whole.' Similarly, Dixon (1993) believes there does not need to be a distinction, but does make a sensible suggestion for clarity, suggesting that leadership is the ability to influence the attitudes and behaviour of others, whilst management is the formal process of decision and command. Visionary leadership is tied to strategic management because as well as needing an overall strategy (direction), a department must pursue the day-to-day operation that gets the job done. In contrast, Torkildsen (1996) believes all successful managers must be leaders and suggests leadership (providing the direction, driving motivation, flexibility and concern for people and results) is one of three crucial tools of management (alongside decision-making and communication). Clearly, it is *what you do* that is most important, rather than becoming a prisoner of terminology.

The Importance of Leadership

> The quality of management . . . is responsible in large measure for the success or failure of the . . . organisation. (Torkildsen, 1996, p. 254)

Departments do not run themselves! Curriculum leaders need a multitude of relevant skills if they are to foster the optimum environment in which improvement, achievement and success can flourish. Leadership is vital as it centres on a concern for people, motivating and managing teams as well as creating appropriate structures to allow all group members to contribute to the fulfilment of an overall plan.

If policy is to be developed and followed, communication and teamwork need to be deliberately facilitated. For a department to achieve its purpose, co-ordination is required to determine who does what, when, where and with whom. Moreover, leaders influence the lives of others, whether this be through influencing people, sharing a vision, developing new policies, applying research to practice, or supporting colleagues. This last point is vital, as 'managing the human component is the most central and important task because all else depends on how well it is done' (Soucie, 1982, p. 191).

Leading others is no easy task. As Handy and Aitkin (1986, p. 47) point out, 'the vagaries of human nature, our urges and inclinations, our defences and fears, our reactions to other people and to authority, all combine to make dealing with people the most puzzling and difficult thing to do in life . . .'. This is one reason why there is a great deal of difference between doing a good job as a teacher (of being responsible *to*) and making others do a good job as a leader (being responsible *for*). Poor personnel management can quickly lead to organizational goal displacement, opposing role expectations and conflict. Leadership, then, represents a process of influencing individuals to work together harmoniously towards achieving identified targets that they endorse. It is also about making the best use of resources that are within one's power. When this is achieved, leadership eliminates inertia, apathy and indifference, replacing them with enthusiasm and conviction as it involves motivating and vitalizing people to contribute maximum effort (Wuest and Bucher, 1995). Furthermore, with so little time to manage, it is important that the head of department is efficient and capable.

The Functions of Leadership

The government is placing ever-increasing managerial demands for detailed information and accountability on schools. The head of department has to think on a broad canvas that requires a breadth of vision and the ability to bring a critical eye to bear on the department. A typical job description for a head of department may include the following responsibilities:

- Keep under review the aims and objectives of the department.
- Co-ordinate work within each year group and review pupil progress and the department's methods of assessment.
- Supervise standards of safety.
- Influence the good appearance of the physical education area.
- Ensure an effective policy towards pupils' behaviour.
- Be responsible for the relevant section of the budget and top manage the resources of the department efficiently.
- Plan and organize courses, expeditions and outings relevant to the work of the department.
- Facilitate a varied extra-curricular programme.
- Advise on staff appointments.
- Ensure high standards of teaching and support colleagues' work.
- Develop and manage sporting links with other education bodies and the wider community.

Such sentiments are reflected in the Teacher Training Agency's (1998) exemplification of the core purpose of the Subject Leader, which highlights the substantial responsibilities of the post:

- The provision of professional leadership and direction for the subject.
- The exemplification of high standards of teaching and learning and the development of appropriate documentation.
- To support, guide and motivate teaching and auxiliary staff.
- To evaluate, monitor and review the effectiveness of current teaching and learning, the curriculum offered and progress towards agreed targets for the pupils and staff.

Raymond (1998) has represented the post of a curriculum leader in terms of two pivotal responsibilities: co-ordination and subject leadership. The realm of co-ordination emphasizes the need to harmonize, work together and establish routines and appropriate practices. The function of subject leadership encapsulates the provision of information, the exhibition of expertise, the offering of direction, and a dedication to raising standards and guidance in the development of the subject.

BAALPE (1999b, p. 15) focuses specifically on four strands of leadership for physical education, 'each of which when fully employed contribute in a balanced way to overall effective subject leadership':

- Visionary (holding a vision for the future of the subject).
- Impact (promoting and generating enthusiasm for physical education).
- Strategic (application of their experience, knowledge and understanding of the physical education curriculum to the planning and delivery of the subject).
- Interpersonal leadership (which 'relies on the Subject Leader having the skills and attributes to ensure effective communication . . . of the ethos, standards, importance and significance of physical education in the school').

The Attributes and Competencies of an Effective Leader

There is no single leadership recipe, nor a definitive set of characteristics that can ensure successful leadership. This is why, according to Weinberg and Gould (1995, p. 203), 'it is easy to think of people who are great leaders, but it is more difficult to determine what makes them leaders'. However, it is quite clear that the leader's personal qualities can have a significant effect, and research into the characteristics and competencies associated with effective leadership reveals a multitude of expected characteristics a leader needs. For clarity, these skills can be categorized into four areas:

- *Hard skills* (e.g., subject knowledge, teaching skills, safety principles).
- *Soft skills* (e.g., understanding of individual and group psychology, communication skills).
- *Conceptual skills* (e.g., practical intelligence, information-processing skills).
- *Personal attributes* (e.g., physical energy, enthusiasm, and warmth).

Hard skills

Technical competence is a good foundation on which to build leadership. It inspires confidence, and those who are being led have a right to expect that leaders will be good at their job. Excellence and experience in teaching means that the head of department has the knowledge and skills to support colleagues and it frees up more time to manage the department. A strong understanding of safety procedures will also help to frame the work of the department and reduce the risk of accidents.

Soft skills

Effective leaders show *concern for the well-being of others* and an awareness of their desires and goals, and they show this support through actions not just words! Research by Smoll and Smith (1989) found that whatever coaching style was used, athletes responded better to supportive coaches rather than punitive ones. Similarly, leaders need to establish effective group and individual peer relationships. They need 'to understand people and the relationships between them . . . without this understanding . . . the manager's chance of successfully and effectively undertaking a task . . . is considerably reduced' (Torkildsen, 1996, p. 287). The leader needs to recognize the strengths and weaknesses of individuals and support them, whilst maintaining group cohesion. Also, recognizing an individual's abilities and contributions will be vital to increase the total effectiveness of the group and foster an individual sense of achievement (Payne, 2000).

Effective leaders deal with distrust and deference (Payne, 2000), so it is essential for the leader to understand *conflict resolution*, and the roots of individual and organizational divisiveness in order to engage with it positively. Group competence and effectiveness often rests on a group regularly evaluating itself and generating different ways of thinking about things:

> Maintaining the group as a cohesive unit with a high level of motivation is a vital aspect . . . It is the role of the leader to ensure, that, when faced with adversity, the group, by its combined effort, can work together to overcome the difficulties. (Keay 1996, p. 12)

Fostering collaboration takes a conscious effort that requires time and energy. Smith (1984) highlights the role of high personal involvement that effective team leaders took in a situation where they had to sort out conflicts and problems in order to make the team more effective. The leader can give support to colleagues through social support and counselling. Team conflict resolution can be built through team-building and improved communication, and by ensuring that the social environment is a pleasant place to work: colleagues are warm and considerate to each other; are interested in the non-work part of colleagues' lives and share social activities. Strong group dynamics are important as better decisions frequently result from the sharing of information and frequent exchanges among members (Soucie, 1982).

Hovelynck and Auweele (1999) highlight the need for leaders to consider group dynamics, and they suggest a number of relevant interactions. The *in-out dimension* is concerned with the social environment of group membership; it analyses who has been rejected or who has isolated themselves from colleagues. The *up–down dimension* considers group members in terms of the influence they exert. Who is dominant and wants to take on the new leader? Who is a follower and may need motivating? The *close–far angle* refers to the relationships between group members: who confides in whom? Who listens to whom or supports someone closely? The *with–against dimension* looks at the quality of the relations between people. Is it positive or negative? Do two people agree a lot and promote enjoyment or are they critical and argumentative of each other? The *forward–backward dimension* adds an important dimension as it considers group members' propensity for changing the dynamics. Individuals can help stimulate the group and encourage development of the group or they can cause stagnation. It is important to keep staff on side as all group members have power to some extent and negatively used it can be problematic (for example, by delaying urgent work, only complying with change superficially or being frequently absent). Hovelynck and Auweele (1999) point out that these dimensions are intended to be descriptive, not evaluative, they simply position people in relation to each other. Conflict is not necessarily harmful as it may be the source of a new idea or help to provide a balanced position, as both sides of an argument are thoroughly aired.

Conceptual skills

Practical intelligence can be understood as a combination of imagination and reasoning powers, or as the ability to appraise situations, to sense relationships between different aspects of a project and draw on past experience to map out a proposed solution. Bennis (1991) suggests that leaders are conceptualizers, able to engage people in formulating effective goals and a vision of what is to be accomplished. A sound level of practical intelligence will also allow the leader to pick up the nuances of the organization and so maximize the processes by which change occurs and goals are achieved.

Decision-making skills lie at the heart of leadership. Heads of department and other leaders spend much of their time shaping and making decisions. So, being able to identify a problem, generate alternative solutions for it, select the best answer and evaluate the outcomes is something that needs to be done properly. Dixon (1993) points out there is a danger that a leader may not evaluate alternatives in sufficient depth because the large number of alternatives makes the task too daunting, the amount of time required for a detailed analysis seems excessive or the uncertainty inherent in forecasting is assumed to make any detailed evaluation pointless. However, a full evaluation is required if the exercise is not to become a pointless one.

Decision-making informs future planning and development, so it is crucial that the former is thoroughly thought out. In this light, a set of criteria to help determine whether the leader has achieved this aim can be set out:

- Identify a wide range of possible solutions.
- Give consideration to the full range of objectives used and the values attached to each choice.
- Carefully weigh up the costs and risks of both the positive and negative consequences of each alternative.
- Diligently search for new information if further evaluation of alternatives is required.
- Accept the new information, even when it does not conform to expectation or the initially preferred choice.
- Revisit the positives and negatives of all the alternatives, before a final decision is made.
- Make detailed plans of the implementation, particularly contingency plans to cope with any expected risks/costs to the chosen path.

(Adapted from Janis and Mann, 1977)

Decision-making skills need to be accompanied by the quality of *decisiveness*. Leaders are expected to get results, so they must make decisions to steer a course of action. Drucker (1955) has advised that when evaluating which alternative to choose to reach an objective, four factors can be used to judge potential solutions:

- Comparing the risk involved to the expected gain.
- Calculating how much effort each alternative involves.
- Calculating the time span involved for each alternative (particularly important if a short-term gain is required).
- Checking the availability of resources to support each alternative.

Communication skills are essential because the head of department is the link between the team, senior management and the community. Lack of communication between the senior management, heads of department and teaching staff can result in confusion over expectations, roles and duties (Jack, 1995), and this can lead to antipathy and disengagement. Good communication, in contrast, helps breed better organization. As Handy and Aitkin (1986) point out, education is an envelope word: it can include almost anything we want, and the department is subject to many people's expectations. As success can be hard to measure, it is vital that the head of department, in discussion with the senior management and colleagues, lays down clearly the objectives of the department.

The leader will also need the potent art of *persuasion*, which relies on effective communication, the ability to control one's own behaviour and empathy for where colleagues 'are coming from'. Communication skills are required as the process by which groups reach decisions is not inevitable and the 'informal structures' of a department can be very useful for the head of department to suggest ideas ahead of a more formal meeting. This may help prevent decisions by minority and no response, which Handy and Aitken (1986) have identified as decisions by mistake.

Productive methods of communicating can include discussions, consultations with individuals or groups, memos, notices, letters, newsletters, official meetings, agendas and minutes of meetings and written reports. When disseminating or seeking information, consulting or negotiating with others, it is vital to select the most appropriate format for communication. For example, in these days of electronic mail (e-mail), leaders must be careful to maintain face-to-face communication, particularly on sensitive issues.

The leader needs to take *responsibility* for the decisions made, even after delegating a task. In physical education, it will obviously be important for the head of department to consider the many safety aspects of the work (e.g., ensuring an adequate risk assessment is conducted on a new scheme of work, and training and supervision are given to staff where required).

A head of department can reflect on some important questions:

- Are procedures sufficiently well organized that staff can be left to get on with their different jobs, but are also free enough to use their initiative?
- Are standards set too low or too high? What are the consequences?
- Am I talking regularly enough with staff, providing praise and constructive criticism (especially for newly qualified teachers)?
- Is the environment friendly, comfortable and mutually supportive? If not, what needs to change to develop this?

Personal attributes

Effective leaders believe in what they are doing; and have a strong *sense of purpose and direction*. They accomplish tasks despite obstacles put in the way by refusing to be side-tracked. Southworth (1998) suggests that good leaders are thought to hold a clear understanding of their own values, beliefs and goals, which should be clear and definite. Having clear goals in physical education is vital as there are not only many expectations on the department but many possible choices of direction to take. Implementation of new ideas do not always happen instantaneously so leaders must be *durable* enough to take an idea through a number of meetings and committees before translating it to operational functioning. Winser (1988, p. 7) suggests leaders need imagination and practicality: 'if you do not have vision you will not start your expedition. But if you do not have realism you will not finish.'

Leaders should exhibit *dependability*. Bennis (1991) believes the 'Management of Trust' (faith in the honesty and reliability of the leader) to be a vital characteristic of effective leadership. Research suggests that effective leaders are consistent in their behaviour and make others feel secure (Dean, 1985). This has led Feldhusen (1994) to conclude that leaders require emotional stability to enable them to think through difficult decisions logically, rather than letting personal feelings dictate choices. Effective leaders have also been found to have a tolerance for high stress (Dean, 1985).

Leaders need qualities of *adaptability and versatility* as the problems to be faced can never be fully predicted, and although new initiatives or developments may be exciting, they can also be the cause of conflict. In physical education, the head of department has to deal with a dual role:

- concern for self as a specialist teacher;
- a manager whose tasks relate to the organization and support of the department.

So, leaders must be able to switch between the two at short notice as they can walk out of a technically difficult lesson one minute, only to be plunged into a staff conflict the next. Furthermore:

> A new . . . head of department, may feel that there are experts on the staff in everything he does well himself and that they don't want interference from a senior colleague. It is sometimes very difficult for someone new in a senior post to come to terms with the fact that some of the skills which made him

successful in a previous post must now be set aside to some extent and he must acquire new skills to meet his new responsibilities. (Dean, 1985, p. 2)

Keeping one's *integrity* is not easy, as a teacher who assumes a managerial position in school has to face what Gross and Herriott (1965) term 'organisational reality': the time when the head of department confronts the complex realities of running the department. This is a time when the teacher has to balance up internalized conceptions of the role with the actual stresses and obligations of the position.

Some aspects of personality or character facilitate taking on the mantle of leadership somewhat easier, as the leader acts as a focal point, drawing different people together to pull in the same direction (Keay, 1996). These qualities are sometimes called *personal impact* or *presence*. 'Referent power' (Coulshed and Mullender, 2001) is closely tied to charisma, in which staff work hard to gain the leader's approval. Soucie (1982) suggests that leadership within a group stems from informal sources of authority, whilst formal authority is power granted by the organization because of the position occupied. Informal authority belongs only to the individual, and stems from characteristics that are outstanding in the personality of the individual, such as sincerity and integrity. Perhaps this is why many schools advertise for a head of department with certain personality characteristics (generosity of spirit, sense of humour, and so on) as well as the organizational ability to run a department.

The head of department needs *self-confidence* to withstand being pulled in different directions by different groups as well as having a foot in different camps. Gross and Herriott (1965) point out that the forces on the leader by people in counter positions (such as the relationship of the head of department to the senior management) will affect relationships with colleagues. If the head of department is seen to be lacking influence, it is likely to have negative effects on the department, as colleagues may have little faith that their efforts will be rewarded. Conversely, leaders have to live with the problem of colleagues' views of their role. Those responsible to the leader have expectations about the style of leadership to be used, and will exert pressure for this to happen.

Styles of Leadership
Effective leaders utilize a variety of styles and strategies depending upon the organizational context and their interpretation of themselves and others in the group. One of the best ways to view management and leadership behaviour is as a continuum (see Figure 10.1).

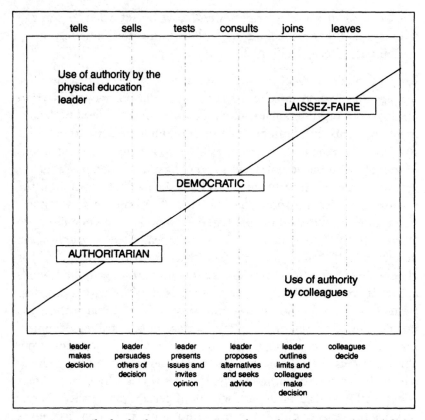

Figure 10.1 *The leadership continuum in physical education* (adapted from Tannenbaum and Schmidt, 1958)

An *authoritarian* leader is task-oriented; someone who places emphasis on getting things done, sometimes at the expense of positive interpersonal relationships (e.g., the leader assesses the situation, selects a course of action and tells the group what to do). Undoubtedly there are advantages to having clear lines of command, coherence and predictable rules, and it helps to make the organization readily answerable to those people it is accountable to. Such leadership can be helpful in certain routine tasks, but is not so suited to teaching with its messiness and unpredictability. Although the department will need to be efficiently designed and structured, the 'exactness' of authoritarian approaches is too rigid; teachers need to be able to use their initiative and adapt quickly to ever-changing daily situations and issues (pupil behaviour, weather; transport; other schools' decisions, and so on). Furthermore, 'one way communication is fraught with difficulties. A does not know if he is getting through to B' (Torkildsen, 1996, p. 279).

The diverse nature of school physical education means that a more flexible framework is needed. The head of department could be away on a field trip or an after-school match when something happens at school that requires immediate action; teachers need the freedom to use their initiative to deal with an issue there and then, rather than having to go through a line manager. Rigid organizational structure can limit teachers' input, when they need to be able to make autonomous judgements.

At the other end of the continuum to the authoritarian leader is *laissez-faire* leadership, typified by a lack of interference and a very relaxed approach, where individuals are trusted to manage relatively independently. When laissez-faire leadership works well, it results in power *with* the members, not power *of* the leader (Wuest and Bucher, 1995). By promoting staff initiative and independence, all teachers act as managers, and so any member of the department can be an instigator of change. Change can come from the inside, and the teacher need not be in a position of power to influence practice. Research suggests that being open to influence will help the head of department be more effective in bringing about change because by including the team in decision-making, the staff will be more committed to the decisions made. Indeed, Cross and Harrison, citing Davies (1995, p. 6) suggest that 'change only occurs when teachers believe in the need for it, know where it is going, are committed to it *and have some ownership of it*' (emphasis added). However, in practice there is a fine line between the laissez-faire leader and no leader at all. Active leadership is usually necessary to prevent inefficiency, a lack of focus and inequity, and to encourage a positive and purposeful working environment.

A *democratic* leader is often more concerned with interpersonal relationships and can be characterized as a relationship-oriented leader (the leader presents the problem and relevant information, the group is consulted to get their ideas on solving it and the leader selects from the alternatives available). This style of leadership aims to keep the lines of communication open, maintain positive social interaction and ensure a feeling of well-being throughout the organization (Weinberg and Gould, 1995). Thus, democratic leadership styles facilitate personal development, confidence and team-building. According to Singer (1976 p. 338):

Persuasive research . . . has revealed that effective leaders do not tend to be dictatorial (authoritarian) or laissez-faire (permissive). Instead, they are democratic; they encourage group members to grow in responsible behaviour, . . . to develop their own ideas, and take responsibility.

Two-way communication is slower and can be frustrating for the sender, but is more sensitive and more accurate, especially in complex situations. It also encourages staff to make use of their abilities, so it has a practical advantage too. For example, in discussing something with a colleague and presenting an argument for change, a staff member may come up with a fact or reason not known or considered by the leader, which prevents a poor judgement. Likert (1967) found that a management system run on 'participative' management principles (which produces decisions by agreement, where the head of department acts rather like a chairperson, to share problems with staff and reach a decision by consensus) led to more positive worker attitudes and higher morale. Conversely, an 'exploitative-authoritative' system produced the opposite effect. In the context of athletics coaching, Usher (1997) found that coaches who followed a prescriptive approach often expressed concern that their athletes suffered from low athlete productivity and motivation and poor performance quality. Drawing on empirical research, Torkildsen (1996) suggests group competence and effectiveness rests on a number of factors, including the high involvement of the group, decisions made mainly by consensus, and the group generating different ways of thinking about things.

By involving other staff more closely in the running of the department, democratic leadership is advantageous in giving the head of department more time to plan ahead and consider the bigger picture. However, delegation (the process by which managers get things done through other people) is a critical skill as too much or too little delegation can irritate staff, so it can be an awkward thing to do. Delegation depends upon a combination of factors including:

- Trusting staff and allowing them to work without interference, but providing sufficient support, where required. However, as delegation always involves the manager retaining oversight of the task, build in checks and balances so people cannot go too far wrong without it becoming apparent.
- Providing the person with the necessary authority to make the decisions required. Non-specific delegation is problematic as it means both parties have to feel their way forward, and leads the 'subordinate' to determine the authority given to them by trial and error.
- Co-ordinating delegation with staff development opportunities

to ensure staff learn from the experience. Delegation, in part, is about coaching and mentoring, so the head of department needs a good understanding of each staff member, including their strengths and weaknesses and current workload. 'Delegation can fruitfully build on staff's own interests but should also challenge people to learn new knowledge and skills; otherwise people will not develop in the rounded way that will equip them to seek advancement in due course' (Coulshed and Mullender, 2001, p. 106).

- Delegating within either the experience or capability of the employee, otherwise a delegated task is only likely to be done poorly, or not at all.
- Heads of department should remember they can also delegate *upwards* since senior managers may have access to resources or experience that will prove beneficial.

Of course, no single style of leadership is without its difficulties and limitations. Democratic approaches tend to centre on issues associated with dealing with a loss of control, managing shared accountability or ensuring that colleagues do not feel unsupported.

The key for leaders would seem to be finding a balance between group participation and maintaining the necessary authority and control over the department for which they are responsible. Only resentment and frustration will ensue from the pretence that the group is being involved. Similarly, giving colleagues responsibility over low-level decisions, whilst maintaining control over the critical ones may also cause problems.

Lofthouse (1994, p. 125) has noted that 'the management of schools has changed from an emphasis upon control, to leadership to bring out the best in people . . .'. Payne (2000) suggests that managers seek group involvement in about two-thirds of situations and overlook the need for group acceptance a third of the time. 'The clever leader is anxious to avoid imposing her or his decision and will therefore strive to sense any emerging consensus so that the members of the group feel that they have some ownership of the final outcome' (Handy and Aitken, 1986, p. 68). However, when staff are given much greater freedom, there is often a need for reassurance and comfort. Buckton (1989, p. 96) reports an interesting example of this in his school's efforts to incorporate children with special needs into the mainstream:

The Educational Psychologist very explicitly abandoned his own role as expert. We responded with flurried outrage, which

changed in time to a really liberating sense of our own competence ... we had a sense that together, with our shared
knowledge of individual children, we were as competent as
anyone else. Thus our anxiety became a strength – it created
propitious conditions for collaboration.

Kidman (2001) has recently suggested the importance of an empowerment approach that provides the staff member with a chance to
be part of the vision and values of the team. It is a person-centred
approach that promotes a sense of belonging, as well as giving the
teacher a role in decision-making and a shared approach to their
professional development. 'Teachers have the authority and are able
to actively engage fully in shaping and defining their own direction'
(Kidman, 2001, p. 14). The advantages of empowerment centre on
the increased motivation to the individual and a greater understanding and retention of what they learn. It may be most useful then
with newly qualified and less experienced teachers supporting the
directives of the Career Entry Profile, and in helping teachers to
move from concern for self to contributing to the wider development
of the department. Taking up this theme, Kaagan (1999, p. xiv)
argues that 'leadership development efforts, if they are ever to have
greater effect, must become more experiential . . .'. In other words,
aspiring leaders need opportunities to experience situations, problems and challenges. He suggests the primary text should be 'shared
experience' as common sense tells us that we learn more through
doing and reflecting on doing than through merely listening. Second,
he points to the importance of professional development through
more formal experience (such as courses) since such experience
allows people time and space to reflect in less precarious circumstances than those of the everyday hurly-burly of school. He appropriately terms this 'safe ground', which is often essential for people
to open themselves up to learning (Kaagan, 1999, p. 13).

Situational Leadership

The leadership continuum reminds us that the leader can relate to
the group in a number of ways: effective leadership is not a matter
of fixed personal style. The different leadership styles can all be
effective, if chosen at the right time for the right group of people.
This has led researchers to consider the importance of the context and
other variables, perhaps because leadership is not exercised in the
abstract, but in the performance of specific tasks (Dean, 1985). The
nature of the situation is perhaps the most important consideration

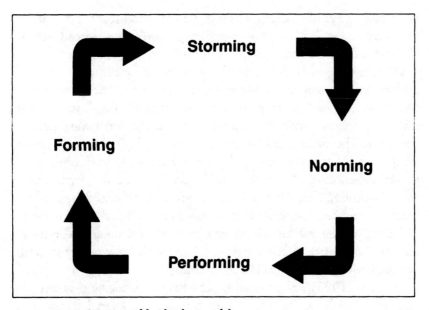

Figure 10.2 *Situational leadership model*

determining the type of leadership required. For instance, it must not be thought that authoritarian leadership is wrong. If the most important thing is to get the job done, such as compliance with the key principles of the National Curriculum before a looming inspection, the head of department may decide to over-ride a normal consultative style in favour of a more command approach. Autocratic leadership is also suitable where a quick response is required, or during an emergency where the leader will have to act fast singularly. For example, if a pupil runs away during sports day, a potentially hazardous situation, the head of department needs to take decisive action. Similarly, where health and safety regulations are required, the head of department can and should insist on set rules and regulations being followed as there is little room for negotiation.

Handy and Aitkin (1986) point out that groups appear to have a clearly defined growth cycle that will affect how the leader works with them. The concept of maturity is a nebulous one, but a group's psychological maturity might be portrayed, for instance, by their willingness to help one another (Coulshed and Mullender, 2001). Hersey and Blanchard (1969) suggest that group development occurs through a series of stages (see Figure 10.2):

When a group is in the *forming* stage, group members evaluate each other. This is often followed by a *storming* period of conflict, either about aims of the group or of individuals. *Norming*, leading to acceptable ways of working and more understood roles and goals, is the third stage. Last comes *performing*, where an agreed set of objectives frames a more mature and productive period.

Different stages of the cycle imply the need for different styles of leadership. For example, when a group reaches the 'storming' phase and wants to start sharing some of the control, the leader might utilize a 'selling' style to explain the reasons for taking certain decisions. The focus switches away from simply 'telling' the group things to a concern for relationships too. For a well-established team leader, a democratic leadership style is possible because, by the time the 'performing' stage is reached, the group is able to debate issues openly, and use arguments to a positive end. The group's maturity and likely desire for high level involvement will mean 'delegation' and shared control is at its greatest. Leadership is low key in both task and relationship fields (Loynes, 1988).

Martens (1987) has proposed that effective leadership is directly related not only to leadership qualities and situational factors but also to member characteristics (the actual attributes of the staff and pupils of a school). Some teachers are happy as simply that and do not want, and may even resent, being given extra responsibility. They see their priority as teaching and resent managerial tasks that may interfere: 'teachers are teachers first and managers when they have to be, because managing is quite clearly a disruptive occupation if you have something else to do' (Handy and Aitkin, 1986, p 36).

A related issue is that of the characteristics of the department and school. How much freedom is the department given by the senior management and what do they expect of the head of department? How do the overall objectives and ethos of the school affect what can be done? Schools vary widely and a variety of management situations will reflect this.

Such a situational view of leadership highlights the need for leaders to be able to select leadership approaches that suit a given circumstance: 'it is impossible to dictate what works best overall or to give one magic set of answers. Everything today is down to flexibility' (Coulshed and Mullender, 2001, p. 100).

Conclusion

One of the most powerful factors contributing to the effective provision of physical education is strong and positive leadership. Curriculum leaders need a multitude of relevant skills if they are to foster the optimum environment in which their department can flourish. There are many different styles and strategies of leadership and the effective leader will be able to move in and out of the various approaches to suit different occasions.

The acid test of leadership is determined by the number of people that it enriches and helps to grow. The head of department needs to consider carefully the opportunities to improve the physical education for all the children in the school, as well as taking colleagues forward, both in terms of supporting these ideals and in forwarding their professional development. Effective leaders develop, so physical education leaders are well advized to experiment with the various leadership approaches so they learn how and when to apply them to their own situation.

References

Alderson, J. and Crutchley, D. (1990) 'Physical Education and the National Curriculum' in Armstrong, N. (ed.), *New Directions in Physical Education, Vol. 1*. Champaign, Ill.: Human Kinetics.

Allison, S. and Thorpe, R. (1997) 'A Comparison of the Effectiveness of Two Approaches to Teaching Games Within Physical Education: a Skills Approach Versus a Games for Understanding Approach', *British Journal of Physical Education*, **28** (3), 9–13.

Almond, L. (1997) *Physical Education in Schools* (2nd edn). London: Kogan Page.

Almond, L. (2000) 'Physical Education and Primary Schools' in Bailey, R. P. and Macfadyen, T. M. (eds), *Teaching Physical Education 5–11*. London: Continuum.

Ames, C. (1992) 'Achievement Goals, Motivational Climate and Motivational Processes' in Roberts, G. C. (ed.), *Motivation in Sport and Exercise*. Champaign, Ill: Human Kinetics.

Ames, C. and Archer, J. (1988) 'Achievement Goals in the Classroom: Students' Learning Strategies and Motivation Processes', *Journal of Educational Psychology*, **80**, 260–7.

Anderson, A. (1999) 'The Case for Learning Strategies in Physical Education', *Journal of Physical Education, Recreation and Dance*, **70** (1), 45–9.

Andrews, J. (1979) *Essays on Physical Education and Sport*. Cheltenham: Stanley Thornes.

Arnold, P. J. (1979) *Meaning in Movement, Sport and Physical Education*. London: Heinemann.

Asher, J. J. (1983) *Learning Another Language Through Actions*. Los Angeles: Sky Oaks.

Aylett, S. (1990) 'Is GCSE at the Crossroads for Physical Education?' *British Journal of Physical Education*, **21** (3), 333–7.

BAALPE (1995) *Safe Practice in Physical Education*. West Midlands: Dudley LEA.

BAALPE (1999a) *Safe Practice in Physical Education – Millennium Edition*. West Midlands: Dudley LEA.

BAALPE (1999b) *Achieving Excellence – Subject Leader in Physical Education*. Exmouth: British Association of Advisers and Lecturers in Physical Education.

Baba, D. (1993) 'Determinants of Video Game Performance', in Starkes, J. C. and Allard, F. (eds) *Cognitive Issues in Motor Expertise*. Amsterdam: Elsevier.

Bailey, R. P. (1999a) 'Play, Health and Physical Development' in David, T. (ed.), *Young Children Learning*. London: Paul Chapman Publishing.

Bailey, R. P. (1999b) 'Physical Education: Action, Play, Movement' in Riley, J. and Prentice, R. (eds), *The Primary Curriculum 7–11*. London: Paul Chapman.

Bailey, R. P. (2000a) *Teaching Values and Citizenship Across the Curriculum*. London: Kogan Page.

Bailey, R. P. (2000b) 'Planning and Preparation for Effective Teaching' in Bailey, R. P. and Macfadyen, T. M. (eds), *Teaching Physical Education 5 –11*. London: Continuum.

Bailey, R. P. (2001a) *Teaching Physical Education: A Handbook for Primary and Secondary Teachers*. London: Kogan Page.

Bailey, R. P. (2001b) 'Learning To Be Human: Teaching, Learning and Human Cognitive Evolution.' Paper presented at the Annual Conference of the British Educational Research Association, Leeds.

Bailey, R. P. and Robertson, C. R. (2000) 'Including All Pupils in Primary School Physical Education' in Bailey, R. P. and Macfadyen, T. M. (eds), *Teaching Physical Education 5–11*. London: Continuum.

Barton, L. (1993) 'Disability, Empowerment and Physical Education' in Evans, J. (ed.), *Equality, Education and Physical Education*. Falmer: London.

Beckett, K. (1990) 'The Effects of Two Teaching Styles on College

Students' Achievement of Selected Physical Education Outcomes,' *Journal of Teaching in Physical Education*, 10, 153–69.

Benn, T. and Benn, B. (1992) *Primary Gymnastics – A Multi-activities Approach*. Cambridge: Cambridge University Press.

Bennis, W. (1991) 'Learning Some Basic Truisms About Leadership', *National Forum: The Phi Kappa Phi Journal*, 71 (1), 12–15.

Biddle, S. (1999) 'The Motivation of Pupils in Physical Education' in Hardy, C. A. and Mawer, M. (eds), *Learning and Teaching in Physical Education*. London: Falmer.

Biddle, S. J. H. and Chatzisarantis, N. (1999) 'Motivation for a Physically Active Lifestyle Through Physical Education' in Vanden Auweele, Y., Bakker, F., Biddle, S., Durand, M. and Biddle, R. (eds), *Psychology for Physical Educators*. Champaign, Ill: Human Kinetics.

Birtwistle, G. and Brodie, D. (1991) 'Children's Attitudes Towards Physical Education', *Health Education Research*, 6, 465–78.

Bjorkvold, J. R. (1989) *The Muse Within – Creativity and Communications, Song and Play from Childhood Through Maturity*. New York: HarperCollins.

Black, K. (1999) 'All Inclusive', *PE and Sport Today*, 1 Winter, 27–9.

Black, K. and Haskins, D. (1996) 'Including all Children in TOP PLAY and BT TOP SPORT', *Primary PE Focus*, Winter, 9–11.

Blamires, M. (1999) 'Universal Design for Learning: Re-establishing Differentiation as part of the Inclusion Agenda', *Support for Learning*, 14 (4), 158–63.

Bloom, B. (1985) *Developing Talent in Young People*. New York: Ballantine.

Booth, T. (1998) 'From "Special Education" To Inclusion and Exclusion in Education. Can We Redefine the Field?' in Haug, P. and Tossebro, J. (eds), *Theoretical Perspectives on Special Education*. Kristians: Hooyskole Forlaget.

Bott, J. (1997) 'Developing Lesson Plans and Units of Work' in Capel, S. (ed.), *Learning to Teach Physical Education in the Secondary School*. London: Routledge.

Boucher, C. A. (1977) 'Education and Accident Prevention – the Work of RoSPA' in Jackson, R. H. (ed.), *Children, the Environment and Accidents*. London: Pitman.

Brady, F. (1998) 'A Theoretical and Empirical Review of the Contextual Interference Effect and the Learning of Motor Skills', *QUEST* 50 (3), 266–93.

Bransford, J. D., Brown, A. L. and Cocking, R. R. *How People Learn*. Washington: National Academy Press.

Brown, M. (1992) 'The Development of Young 5,000-metre Runners', *Athletics Coach*, **26** (2), 10–14.

Brown, M. and Gordon, W. A. (1987) 'Impact of Impairment on Activity Patterns of Children', *Archives of Physical Medicine and Rehabilitation*, **68**, 828–32.

Brown, S. (1994) 'Assessment: a Changing Practice' in Moon, B. and Mayes, A. S. (eds), *Teaching and Learning in the Secondary School*. London: Routledge/Open University.

Browne, J. (1988) 'Gender Equity Issues in the Assessment of Physical Education in Sex-Integrated Classes,' *ACHPER National Journal*, September, 19–29.

Bruner, J. (1983) *Child's Talk: Learning to Use Language*. Oxford: Oxford University Press.

Bucher, C. A. and Thaxton, N. A. (1981) *Physical Education and Sport: Change and Challenge*. St Louis: C. V. Mosby.

Buckton, C. (1989) 'Teamwork in the Primary School' in Bowers, T. (ed.) *Managing Special Needs*. Milton Keynes: Open University Press.

Bunker, D. (1994) *Primary Physical Education – Implementing the National Curriculum*, Cambridge: Cambridge University Press.

Capel, S., Kelly, L. and Whitehead, M. (1997) 'Developing and Maintaining an Effective Learning Environment' in Capel, S. (ed.), *Learning to Teach Physical Education in the Secondary School*. London: Routledge.

Capel, S. (2000a) 'Re-reflecting on Priorities for Physical Education: Now and in the Twenty-First Century' in Capel, S. and Piotrowski, S. (eds) *Issues in Physical Education*. London: Routledge/Falmer.

Capel, S. (2000b) 'Approaches to Teaching Games' in Capel, S. and Piotrowski, S. (eds) *Issues in Physical Education*, London: Routledge/Falmer.

Carlson, T. (1995) 'Now I think I can'. The Reaction of Low Skilled Students to Sports Education', *ACHPER Healthy Lifestyles Journal*, **42** (4), 6–8.

Carroll, B. (1994) *Assessment in Physical Education: A Teacher's Guide to the Issues*. London: Falmer.

Carroll, B. (1998) 'The Emergence and Growth of Examinations in Physical Education' in Green, K. and Hardman, K. (eds) *Physical Education: A Reader*. Aachen: Meyer and Meyer.

Casbon, C. (1988) 'Examinations in PE – A Path to Curriculum

Development', *British Journal of Physical Education*, **19** (6), 217–19.

CCW (1992) *Physical Education in the National Curriculum*. Cardiff: Curriculum Council for Wales.

Ceci, S. and Williams, W. (1999) *The Nature–Nurture Debate: The Essential Readings*. Oxford: Blackwell.

Clark, C. M. and Yinger, R. J. (1987) 'Teacher Planning' in Calderhead, J. (ed.), *Exploring Teachers' Thinking*. London: Cassell.

Clay, G. (1997) 'Standards in Primary and Secondary Physical Education: OfSTED 1995–6', *British Journal of Physical Education*, **28** (2), 5–9.

Cleland, F. E. (1994) 'Young Children's Divergent Movement Ability: Study II', *Journal of Teaching in Physical Education*, **13** (3), 228–41.

Coakley, J. J. and White, A. (1992) 'Making Decisions: Gender and Sport Participation Among British Adolescents', *Sociology of Sport Journal*, 9, 20–35.

Cockburn, C. (2001) 'Year 9 Girls and Physical Education: A Survey of Pupil Perception', *Bulletin of Physical Education*, **37** (1), 5–24.

Cohen, L., Manion, L. and Morrison, K. (1996) *A Guide to Teaching Practice*. London: Routledge.

Coleman, J. A. (1961) *The Adolescent Society*. New York: Free Press.

Cooper, P. (1996) 'Giving it a Name: The Value of Descriptive Categories in Educational Approaches to Emotional and Behavioural Difficulties', *Support for Learning*, **11** (4), 146–50.

Corbett, J. (1995) *Bad Mouthing*. London: Routledge.

Coulshed, V. and Mullender, A. (2001) *Management in Social Work* (2nd edn). Basingstoke: Palgrave.

Csikszentmihalyi, M. (1975) *Beyond Boredom and Anxiety*. San Francisco: Jossey-Bass.

Curtner-Smith, M. and Hasty, D. L. (1997) 'Influence of National Curriculum Physical Education on Teacher's Use of Teaching Styles', *Research Quarterly for Exercise and Sport: Supplement*, **68** (1), A-75–A-76.

Cutter, S. L. (1993) *Living with Risk*. London: Edward Arnold.

Daley, D. (1988) 'GCSE PE and the Bilingual Child', *British Journal of Physical Education*, **19** (6), 222–3.

Davies, J. (1995) *Developing a Leadership Role in Key Stage 1 Curriculum*. London: Falmer.

Dean, J. (1985) *Managing the Secondary School*. London: Croon Helm.

Department for National Heritage (DNH) (1995) *Sport: Raising the Game*. London: DNH.

DES (1978) *Special Educational Needs (Warnock Report)*. London: HMSO.

DES (1980) *Safety in Physical Education* (Safety series no. 4). London: HMSO.

DES (1988) *The New Teacher in School: A Survey by HM Inspectors in England and Wales, 1987*. London: HMSO.

DES (1989) *Records of Achievement. Report of the ROA National Steering Committee* (RANSC). London: DES.

DES/WO (1989) *Discipline in Schools (The Elton Report)*. London: HMSO.

DES/WO (1992) *Physical Education: The National Curriculum for England and Wales*. London: HMSO.

DFE (1994) *The Code of Practice on the Identification and Assessment of Special Educational Needs*. London: Department for Education.

DfEE (1997) *Excellence for all Children: Meeting Special Educational Needs* (Green Paper). London: Stationery Office.

DfEE (1998) *Meeting Special Educational Needs: a Programme of Action*. London: DfEE.

DfEE/QCA (1999) *Physical Education. The National Curriculum for England*. London: DfEE and QCA.

DfES (2001) Excellence in Cities Project: http://www.standards.dfes.gov.uk/excellence/ig_gtc_.html

Dickenson, B. and Almond, L. (1987) 'Accreditation: Part II: Issues for P.E.', *British Journal of Physical Education*, 18 (4), 175–6.

Dixon, R. (1993) *The Management Task*. Oxford: Butterworth-Heinemann Ltd.

Drucker, P. F. (1955) *The Practice of Management*. London: Heinemann.

Dweck, C. S. (1986) 'Motivational Processes Affecting Learning,' *American Psychologist*, 41, 1040–8.

Eastwood, P. and Buswell, J. (1987) 'Education and Training for Leadership in P.E.', *The Bulletin of Physical Education*, 23 (2), 35–7.

Ericsson, K. A., Krampe, R. and Tesch-Romer, C. (1993) 'The Role of Deliberate Practice in the Acquisition of Expert Performance', *Psychological Review*, 100, 363–406.

Evans, J., Penney, D. and Davies, B. (1996a) 'Back to the Future: Education Policy and Physical Education' in Armstrong, N. (ed.),

New Directions in Physical Education: Change and Innovation. London: Cassell.

Evans, J., Davies, B. and Penney, D. (1996b) 'Teachers, Teaching and the Social Construction of Gender Relations', *Sport, Education and Society*, **1** (2) 165–83.

Eve, N. (1997) 'Safe Practice in Physical Education: Some Notes from the Safety Officer', *Bulletin of Physical Education*, **33** (3), 30–2.

Eyre, D. (1994) *Able Children in Ordinary Schools*. London: David Fulton.

Eyre, D. and Marjoram, T. (1990) *Enriching and Extending the National Curriculum*. London: Kogan Page.

Fairclough, S. and Stratton, G. (1997) 'Physical Education Curriculum and Extra Curriculum Time: A Survey of Secondary Schools in the North-West of England', *British Journal of Physical Education*, **28** (3), 21–4.

Feldhusen, J. F. (1994) 'Learning and Cognition of Talented Youth' in Van Tassel-Baska, J. (ed.) *Comprehensive Curriculum for Gifted Learners*. Massachusetts: Allyn and Bacon.

Fernandez-Balboa, J. M. (1991) 'Beliefs, Interactive Thoughts, and Actions of Physical Education Student Teachers Regarding Pupil Misbehaviours', *Journal of Teaching Physical Education*, **11** (1), 59–78.

Fisher, C., Berliner, D., Filby, N., Marliave, R., Cahen, L. and Dishaw, M. (1980) 'Teaching Behaviors, Academic Learning Time, and Student Achievement: an Overview' in Denham, C. and Lieberman, A. (eds), *Time to Learn*. Washington DC: National Institute of Education.

Flintoff, A. (1991) 'Equal Opportunities and Practical Assessment in Examination P.E: Part 2', *British Journal of Physical Education*, **22** (1), 35–7.

Flintoff, A. (1998) 'Sexism and Homophobia in Physical Education: the Challenge for Teacher Education' in Green, K. and Hardman, K. (eds), *Physical Education: a Reader*. Aachen: Meyer and Meyer.

Fox, K. (1988) 'The Child's Perspective in Physical Education I: The Psychological Dimension in Physical Education', *British Journal of Physical Education*, **19** (1), 34–8.

Francis, J. (1992) 'The Growth, Development and Future of Physical Education and Sports Studies at Advanced Level GSCE', *British Journal of Physical Education*, **23** (1), 35–7.

Francis, J. and Merrick, I. (1994) 'The Future of A Level Physical

Education and Sport Studies', *British Journal of Physical Education*, **25** (3), 13–16.

Freeman, J. (1983) 'Identifying the Able Child' in Kerry, T. (ed.) *Finding and Helping the Able Child*. Beckenham: Croon Helm.

Freeman, J. (1998) *Educating the Very Able: Current International Research*. London: OfSTED.

Gagne, F. (1985) 'Giftedness and Talent: Re-examining a Re-examination of the Definitions', *Gifted Child Quarterly*, **29** (3), 103–12.

Gallahue, D. (1993) *Developmental Physical Education for Today's Children*. Madison, WI: Brown and Benchmark.

Gardner, H. (1983) *Frames of Mind: the Theory of Multiple Intelligences*. New York: Basic Books.

Glass, R., Christiansen, J. and Christiansen, J. L. (1982) *Teaching Exceptional Children in the Regular Classroom*. Boston: Little, Brown and Co.

Gildenhuys, C. A. and Orsmond, C. P. (1996) 'Movement and Second Language Acquisition: the Potential and the Method', *Sport, Education and Society*, **1** (1), 103–15.

Gipps, C. and Stobart, G. (1993) *Assessment: a Teacher's Guide to the Issues*. London: Falmer.

Goldberger, M. (1992) 'The Spectrum of Teaching Styles: A Perspective for Research on Teaching Physical Education', *Journal of Physical Education, Recreation and Dance*, **63** (1), 42–6.

Goldberger, M. (1995) 'Research on the Spectrum of Teaching Styles' in Lidor, R., Eldar, E. and Harari, I. (eds), *Windows to the Future: Bridging the Gaps Between Disciplines, Curriculum and Instruction*. Proceedings of the 1995 AIESEP World Congress, Part II, Wingate Institute for Physical Education and Sport, Israel, 429–35.

Good, T. L. and Brophy, J. E. (1991) *Looking at Classrooms*. New York: HarperCollins.

Goudas, M. and Biddle, S. (1994) 'Perceived Motivational Climate and Intrinsic Motivation in School Physical Education Classes' *European Journal of Psychology of Education*, **9**, 241–50.

Goudas, M., Biddle, S., Fox, K. and Underwood, M. (1995) 'It ain't what you do, it's the way that you do it! Teaching Style Affects Children's Motivation in Track and Field Lessons' *The Sports Psychologist*, **9**, 254–64.

Grant, B. (1992) 'Integrating Sport into the Physical Education Curriculum in New Zealand Schools', *Quest*, **44** (3), 304–16.

Grineski, S. (1996) *Co-operative Learning in Physical Education.* Champaign, Ill.: Human Kinetics.

Gross, J. (1996) *Special Educational Needs in the Primary School* (2nd edn). Milton Keynes: Open University Press.

Gross, M. U. M. (1993) *Exceptionally Gifted Children.* London: Routledge.

Gross, N. and Herriott, R. E. (1965) *Staff Leadership in Public Schools: A Sociological Inquiry.* New York: John Wiley and Sons.

Handy, C. and Aitken, R. (1986) *Understanding Schools as Organizations.* Bungay, Suffolk: Richard Clay (The Chaucer Press).

Hardman, K. and Marshall, J. J. (2001) 'Worldwide Survey on the State and Status of Physical Education in Schools' in Doll-Tepper, G. and Scoretz, D. (eds), *World Summit on Physical Education.* Berlin: ICSSPE.

Hardy, C. (1999) 'Student Misbehaviours and Teachers' Responses in Physical Education Lessons' in Hardy, C. and Mawer, M. (eds), *Learning and Teaching in Physical Education,* London: Falmer.

Harlen, W., Gipps, C., Broadfoot, P. and Nuttall, D. (1994) 'Assessment and the Improvement of Education' in Moon, B. and Mayes, A. S. (eds), *Teaching and Learning in the Secondary School,* London: Routledge/Open University Press.

Harris, J. (1994) 'Physical Education in the National Curriculum: Is there Enough Time to be Effective' *British Journal of Physical Education,* **25** (4), 34–8.

Harris, J. (1998) *The Nurture Assumption.* London: Bloomsbury.

Harrison, J. M., Fellingham, G. W., Buck, M. M. and Pellett, T. L. (1995) 'Effects of Practice and Command Styles on Rate of Change in Volleyball Performance and Self-efficacy of High, Medium, and Low Skilled Learners', *Journal of Teaching in Physical Education,* **14**, 328–39.

Harrison, P. and Watkins, J. (1996) 'Legal Considerations for Teachers and Instructors', *British Journal of Physical Education,* **27** (2), 20–2.

Haug, P. and Tossebro, J. (eds) (1998) *Theoretical Perspectives on Special Education.* Hooyskole Forlaget: Kristians.

Hayes, S. and Sidder, G. (1999) 'A Survey of Physical Education Trainees' Experiences on School Placements in the South-east of England 1994–1998', *British Journal of Teaching Physical Education,* **30** (10), 28–32.

Hayward, K. M. (1993) *Life Span Motor Development,* Champaign, Ill: Human Kinetics.

HEA (Health Education Authority) (1997) *Young People and Physical Activity: A Literature Review.* London: HEA.

Headington, R. (2000) *Monitoring, Assessment, Recording, Reporting and Accountability.* London: David Fulton.

Hellison, D. R. and Templin, T. J. (1991) *A Reflective Approach to Teaching Physical Education.* Champaign, Ill.: Human Kinetics.

Helsen, W. F., Hodges, N. J., Van Winckel, J. and Starkes, J. L. (2000) 'The Roles of Talent, Physical Precocity and Practice in the Development of Soccer Expertise,' *Journal of Sports Sciences,* 18, 727–36.

Henderson, S. and Sugden, D. (1992) *Movement Assessment Battery for Children.* Sidcup: Psychological Corporation.

Hersey, P. and Blanchard, K. H. (1969) *Management of Organizational Behaviour.* New York: Prentice Hall.

Hildreth, G. H. (1966) *Introduction to the Gifted.* New York: McGraw Hill.

Hill, M. S. and Hill, F. W. (1994) *Creating Safe Schools – What Principals Can Do.* California: Corwin Press.

HMI (1992) *The Education of Very Able Children in Maintained Schools – A Review by HMI.* London: HMSO.

HMI (1993) *The Education of Able Pupils.* Edinburgh: Scottish Office Education Dept.

Hodgson, B. (1996) 'Which Exam?', *British Journal of Physical Education,* 27 (2), 23–6.

Hopper, B., Grey, J. and Maude, T. (2000) *Teaching Physical Education in the Primary School.* London: Routledge/Falmer.

Housner, L. (1990) 'Selecting Master Teachers: Evidence from the Process-Product Research', *Journal of Teaching in Physical Education,* 9 (3), 201–26.

Hovelynck, J. and Auweele, Y. A. (1999) 'Group Development in the Physical Education Class' in Auweele, Y. A., Bakker, F., Biddle, S., Durand, M. and Seiler, R. (eds), *Psychology for Physical Educators.* Champaign, Ill.: Human Kinetics.

Howe, M. J. A., Davidson, J. W. and Sloboda, J. A. (1998) 'Innate Talents: Reality or Myth' *Behavioral and Brain Sciences,* 21, 399–442.

Jack, S. (1995) 'Improving the Effectiveness of the Physical Education Curriculum Leader in Primary Schools', *Primary PE Focus,* Autumn Edition, 4–5.

Janis, I. and Mann, F. (1977) *Decision Making.* London: Free Press.

Jenkinson, J. C. (1997) *Mainstream or Special: Educating Students with Disabilities.* London: Routledge.

Johnson, D. W. and Johnson, R. T. (1975) *Learning Together and Alone: Co-operation, Competition and Individualization*. New York: Prentice Hall.

Jowsey, S. (1992) *Can I Play Too? Physical Education for Physically Disabled Children in Mainstream Schools*. London: David Fulton.

Joyce, B. and Weil, M. (1986) *Models of Teaching*. Englewood Cliffs, N.J: Prentice Hall.

Kaagan, S. (1999) *Leadership Games*. Thousand Oaks, Ca.: Sage.

Kaplan, P. S. (1996) *Pathways for Exceptional Children*. St Paul, MN: West.

Kay, T. (1995) *Women and Sport: a Review of Research*. London: Sports Council.

Keay, W. (1996) *The Duke of Edinburgh's Award: Expedition Guide*. Windsor: The Duke of Edinburgh's Award.

Keighley, P. (1993) 'A Consideration of the Appropriate, Learning and Assessment Strategies in the Outdoor Adventurous Activity Element of Outdoor Education as it Relates to the Physical Education National Curriculum', *British Journal of Physical Education*, **24** (1), 18–22.

Kelly, L. (1997) 'Safety in PE' in Capel, S. (ed.) *Learning to Teach Physical Education in the Secondary School*. London: Routledge.

Kidman, L. (2001) *Developing Decision Makers*. Christchurch, NZ: Innovative Print Communications Ltd.

Kinchin, G., Penney, D. and Clarke, G. (2001) 'Teaching the National Curriculum Physical Education: Try Sport Education', *British Journal of Physical Education*, **32** (2), 41–4.

Kizer, D. L., Piper, D. L. and Sauter, W. E. (1984) *A Practical Approach to Teaching Physical Education*. New York: Movement Publications.

Kyriacou, C. (1991) *Essential Teaching Skills*. Hemel Hempstead: Simon and Schuster.

Lambirth, A. and Bailey, R. P. (2000) 'Promoting a Positive Learning Environment' in Bailey, R. P. and Macfadyen, T. M. (eds), *Teaching Physical Education 5–11*. London: Continuum.

Lave, J. (1988) *Cognition in Practice*. Cambridge: Cambridge University Press.

Laws, C. and Fisher, R. (1999) 'Pupils' Interpretation of Physical Education' in Hardy, C. and Mawer, M. (eds), *Learning and Teaching in Physical Education*. London: Falmer.

Leyden, S. (1990). *Helping the Pupil of Exceptional Ability*. London: Routledge.

Lickert, R. (1967) *The Human Organization*. New York: McGraw Hill.

Lockwood, A. (2000) 'Breadth and Balance in the Physical Education Curriculum' in Capel, S. and Piotrowski, S. (eds), *Issues in Physical Education*. London: Routledge/Falmer.

Lofthouse, M. (1994) 'Managing Learning' in Bush, T. and West-Burnham, J. (eds), *The Principles of Educational Management*, Harlow: Longmans.

Loynes, C. (1988) *Expedition Leadership* in Winser, N. and Winser, S. (eds) *Expedition Planners' Handbook and Directory 1988/89*. London: Expedition Advisory Centre.

Macfadyen, T. (1999) 'An Analysis of the Influence of Secondary School Physical Education on Young People's Attitudes Towards Physical Activity', *Bulletin of Physical Education*, **35** (3), 157–72.

Macfadyen, T. (2000) 'The Effective Use of Teaching Styles' in Bailey, R. P. and Macfadyen, T. M. (eds) *Teaching Physical Education 5–11*. London: Continuum.

Macfadyen, T. and Osborne, M. (2000) 'Teaching Games' in Bailey, R. and Macfadyen, T. (eds), *Teaching Physical Education 5–11*. London: Continuum.

Macfadyen, T. M., Bailey, R. P., and Osborne, M. (2000) 'Teaching Athletics', in Bailey, R. and Macfadyen, T. (eds), *Teaching Physical Education 5–11*. London: Continuum.

MacKreth, K. (1998) 'Developments in "A" Level Physical Education', *British Journal of Physical Education*, **29** (4), 16–17.

MacPhail, A. (2000) 'Pupils' Subject Choice: Higher Grade Physical Education', *The British Journal of Teaching Physical Education*, **31** (4), 42–5.

Malina, R. M. and Bouchard, C. (1991) *Growth, Maturation and Physical Activity*, Champaign, Ill.: Human Kinetics.

Maltby, F. (1984) *Gifted Children and Teachers in the Primary School 5–12*. London: Falmer.

Marjoran, T. (1988) *Teaching Able Children*. London: Kogan Page.

Martens, R. (1987) *Coaches Guide to Sports Psychology*. Champaign, Ill.: Human Kinetics.

Mason, V. (1995) *A National Survey: Young People in Sport in England 1994*. London: Sports Council.

Mawer, M. (1995) *The Effective Teaching of Physical Education*. London: Longman.

Mawer, M. (1999) 'Teaching Styles and Teaching Approaches in Physical Education: Research Developments' in Hardy, C. A. and

Mawer, M. (eds), *Learning and Teaching in Physical Education*. London: Falmer.

McConachie-Smith, J. (1996) 'Physical Education at Key Stage 4' in Armstrong, N. (ed.), *New Directions in Physical Education*. London: Cassell.

Meakin, D. (1982) 'Physical Education: an Agency for Moral Education', *Journal of Philosophy of Education*, 15 (2), 241–54.

Metzler, M. (1989) 'A Review of Research on Time in Sport Pedagogy', *Journal of Teaching in Physical Education*, 8 (2), 87–103.

Milosevic, L. (1996) 'Pupils' Experience of PE – Questionnaire Results, *British Journal of Physical Education*, 27 (1), 16–20.

Mittler, P. (2000) *Moving Towards Inclusive Education: Social Contexts*. London: David Fulton.

Montgomery, D. (1996). *Educating the Able*. London: Cassell.

Moon, S. M., Feldhusen, J. F. and Dillon, D. R. (1994) 'Long-term Effects of an Enrichment Program based on the Purdue Three-stage Model', *Gifted Pupil Quarterly*, 38, 38–48.

Morris, H. (1991) 'The Role of School Physical Education in Public Health' *Research Quarterly for Exercise and Sport*, 62 (2), 143–7.

Mortimore, P., Sammons, P., Stoll, L., Lewis, D. and Ecob, R. (1994) 'Teacher Expectations' in Moon, B. and Mayes, A. S. (eds), *Teaching and Learning in the Secondary School*. London: Routledge/Open University.

Mosston, M. (1992) 'Tug-O-War, No More: Meeting Teaching-Learning Objectives using the Spectrum of Teaching Styles', *Journal of Physical Education Recreation and Dance*, 63 (1), 27–31, 56.

Mosston, M. and Ashworth, S. (1986) *Teaching Physical Education*. Columbus, OH: Merrill.

Murphy, C. (1990) 'Who'd Tackle GCSE PE?', *British Journal of Physical Education*, 21 (3), 341–3.

National Association of Head Teachers (NAHT) (1999) Press Release: *NAHT Publishes the Results of its Survey of PE and Sports in Schools*, 4 March 1999.

NCC (1992) *Physical Education: Non-statutory Guidance*. York: National Curriculum Council.

NCET (1993) *Differentiating the School Curriculum*, Wiltshire: Wiltshire LEA.

NCF (National Coaching Foundation) (1986) *Safety First for Coaches*. Leeds: National Coaching Foundation.

Nicholls, J. (1984) 'Conceptions of Ability and Achievement Motivation' in Ames, K. and Ames, C. (eds), *Research on Motivation in Education: Vol. 1: Student Motivation*. New York: Academic Press.

Nixon, H. E. and Jewett, A. E. (1974) *An Introduction to Physical Education*. Philadelphia: Saunders.

Norwich, B. (1990) *Reappraising Special Educational Needs*. London: Cassell.

Norwich, B. (1996) 'Special Needs Education or Education for All: Connective Specialization or Ideological Impurity?' *British Journal of Special Education*, **3**, 100–4.

Norwich, B. (1999) 'Review Article: Special or Inclusive Education?', *European Journal of Special Needs Education*, **14** (1), 90–6.

O'Connor, M. (1987) *Out and About – Teachers' Guide to Safe Practice Out of School*. London: Routledge.

OfSTED (1995) *Physical Education: A Review of Inspection Findings 1993–94*. London: HMSO.

OfSTED (1995a) *Physical Education and Sport in Schools: a Review of Good Practice*. London: HMSO.

OfSTED (1998) *Secondary Education 1993–97: A Review of Secondary Schools in England*. London: HMSO.

OfSTED (2001) *Secondary Education 1993–97: A Review of Secondary Education Schools in England*, http://www.official-documents.co.uk/document/ofsted/seced/chap-5a.htm; & 7k.htm

OHMCI (Office of Her Majesty's Chief Inspector) (1998) *Standards and Quality in Primary Schools – Good Practice in Physical Education and Sport*. London: HMSO.

Oliver, M. (1990) *The Politics of Disablement*. Basingstoke: Macmillan.

Oliver, M. (1996) *Understanding Disability: From Theory to Practice*. Basingstoke: Macmillan.

Owen, J. (1968) 'Physical Education and Needs of the Secondary School Child', *Bulletin of Physical Education*, Conference Supplement.

Papaioannou, A. and Goudas, M. (1999) 'Motivational Climate of the Physical Education Class' in Vanden Auweele, Y., Bakker, F., Biddle, S., Durand, M. and Seiler, R. (eds), *Psychology for Physical Educators*. Champaign, Ill.: Human Kinetics.

Parry, J. (1998) 'The Justification of Physical Education' in Green, K. and Hardman, K. (eds), *Physical Education Reader*. Aachen: Meyer and Meyer Sport.

Payne, M. (2000) *Teamwork in Multiprofessional Care*. Basingstoke: Macmillan Press.

PEA (Physical Education Association), (1995) *Teaching Physical Education at Key Stages 1 and 2*. London: PEA UK.

PEA (Physical Education Association) (1998) PEA UK Mission Statements, *British Journal of Physical Education*, **29** (2), 4–7.

Penney, D. and Evans, J. (1994) 'It's Just Not (and Not Just) Cricket', *British Journal of Physical Education*, **25** (3), 9–12.

Penney, D. and Evans, J. (1997) 'Naming the Game. Discourse and Domination in Physical Education and Sport in England and Wales', *European Physical Education Review*, **3** (1), 21–32.

Perkins, J. (1997) Safety Issues for Pupils with Special Educational Needs in Mainstream Schools, *The Bulletin of Physical Education*, **33** (3), 33–41.

Peters, R. S. (1966) *Ethics and Education*, London: Allyn and Unwin.

Pieron, M. (1998) 'A Review of the Literature in English on Instruction During the Years 1994–95', *International Journal of Physical Education* **35** (1), 5–16.

Piotrowski, S. (2000) 'Assessment, Recording and Reporting' in Bailey, R. P. and Macfadyen, T. M. (eds), *Teaching Physical Education 5–11*. London: Continuum.

Placek, J. H. (1983) 'Conceptions of Success in Teaching: Busy, Happy and Good' in Templin, T. J. and Olson, J. (eds), *Teaching in Physical Education*, Champaign, Ill.: Human Kinetics.

Prochaska, J. O. and Marcus, B. H. (1994) 'The Transtheoretical Model: Applications to Exercise' in Dishman, R. K. (ed.) *Exercise Adherence II*. Champaign, Ill.: Human Kinetics.

Pye, J. (1988) *Invisible Children*. Oxford: Oxford University Press.

QCA (1999) *Terminology in Physical Education*. London: Qualification and Curriculum Authority.

Raymond, C. (1998) *Co-ordinating Physical Education Across the Primary School*. London: Falmer.

Read, B. and Edwards, P. (1992) *Teaching Children to Play Games 5–11: A Resource for Primary Teachers*. Leeds: NCF/BCPE/Sports Council.

Renzulli, J. S. (1995) 'New Directions for the School-wide Enrichment Model' in Katzko, M. W. and Monks, F. J. (eds) *Nurturing Talent: Individual Needs and Social Ability*. Assen, NL: Van Gorcum.

Renzulli, J. S. and Reis, S. M. (1991) 'The School-wide Enrichment Model: a Comprehensive Plan for the Development of Creative

Productivity' in Colangelo, N. and Davis, G. A. (eds) *Handbook of Gifted Education*. Massachusetts: Allyn and Bacon.

Richert, E. S. (1991) 'Rampant Problems and Promising Practices in Identification' in Colangelo, N. and Davis, G. A. (eds) *Handbook of Gifted Education*. Needham Heights, Mass.: Allyn and Bacon.

Rink, J. E. (1993) *Teaching Physical Education for Learning*. St. Louis, MI: Mosby.

Rink, J. E. (1999) 'Instruction from a Learning Perspective' in Hardy, C. A. and Mawer, M. (eds) *Learning and Teaching in Physical Education*. London: Falmer.

Ripley, K., Daines, B. and Barrett, J. (1997) *Dyspraxia: a Guide for Teachers and Parents*. London: David Fulton.

Roberts, G. (1992) 'Motivation in Sport and Exercise: Conceptual Constraints and Conceptual Convergence' in Roberts, G. (ed.) *Motivation in Sport and Exercise*, Champaign, Ill.: Human Kinetics.

Roberts, G. and Treasure, D. (1993) 'The Importance of the Study of Children in Sport: an Overview' in Lee, M. (ed.), *Coaching Children in Sport – Principles and Practice*. London: E. & F. N. Spon.

Roberts, K. (1996) 'Young People, School Sport and Government Policies', *Sport, Education and Society*, 1 (1), 47–59.

Robertson, C. R. (1999a) 'Early Intervention: the Education of Young Children with Developmental Co-ordination Disorder (DCD)' in David, T. (ed.) *Young Children Learning*. London: Paul Chapman.

Robertson, C. R. (1999b) *Equality and the Inclusion of Pupils with Special Educational Needs in Physical Education*. Paper presented at SERA Annual Conference, October 1999, University of Dundee.

Robertson, J. (1989) *Effective Classroom Control*. London: Hodder and Stoughton.

Rowland, T. W. (1991) 'Is There a Scientific Rationale Supporting the Value of Exercise for the Present and Future Cardiovascular Health of Children? The Con Argument', *Pediatric Exercise Science*, 8, 303–9.

Rowlands, P. (1974) *Gifted Children and Their Problems*. London: Dent and Sons.

Ruddock, J., Harris, S. and Wallace, G. (1994) 'Coherence and Students' Experience of Learning in the Secondary School', *Cambridge Journal of Education*, 24, 197–213.

Sallis, J. and Mckenzie, T. (1991) 'PE's role in Public Health', *Research Quarterly for Exercise and Sport*, **62** (2), 124–37.

Sarrazin, P. and Famose, J. -P. (1999) 'Children's Goals and Motivation in Physical Education' in Vanden Auweele, Y., Bakker, F., Biddle, S., Durand, M. and Seiler, R. (eds), *Psychology for Physical Educators*. Champaign, Ill.: Human Kinetics.

Saunders, M. (1979) *Class Control and Behaviour Problems: a Guide for Teachers*. Maidenhead: McGraw-Hill.

Sayler, M. (1999) *Giftedness and Talent: What Do They Mean?* http://www.coe.ent.edu/auxill/its/5150/definitions/sld001.htm

SCAA (1995) *Planning the Curriculum at Key Stages 1 and 2*. London: SCAA.

Schmidt, R. (1983) *Motor Control and Learning: A Behavioral Emphasis*. Champaign, Ill.: Human Kinetics.

Scott, T. (1997) 'Key Stage 4 GCSE in PE', *British Journal of Physical Education*, **28** (2), 14–16.

SEAC (Schools Examination and Assessment Council) (1992) *Teacher Assessment at Key Stage 3*. London: SEAC.

Sharp, R. and Green, A. (1975) *Education and Social Control: A Study in Progressive Primary Education*. London: Routledge and Kegan Paul.

Shields, D. L. L. and Bredemeier, B. J. L. (1995) *Character Development and Physical Education*. Champaign, Ill.: Human Kinetics.

Siedentop, D. (1991) *Developing Teaching Skills in Physical Education (3rd edn)*. Palo Alto, CA: Mayfield.

Siedentop, D. (1994) *Sport Education: Quality PE Through Positive Sport Experiences*. Champaign, Ill.: Human Kinetics.

Silverman, S. (1991) 'Research on Teaching in Physical Education', *Research Quarterly for Exercise and Sport*, **62** (4), 352–64.

Singer, R. N. (1976) *Physical Education: Foundations*. New York: Holt, Rinehart and Winston.

Smith, P. (1984) 'Social Service Teams and Their Managers', *British Journal of Social Work*, **16** (6), 601–13.

Smoll, F. L. and Smith, R. E. (1989) 'Leadership Behaviors in Sport: a Theoretical Model and Research Paradigm', *Journal of Applied Social Psychology*, **19** (18), 1522–51.

Snow, R. E. (1989) 'Aptitude Treatment Interaction as a Framework for Research on Individual Differences in Learning' in Ackerman, P., Sternberg, R. and Glaser, R. (eds) *Learning and Individual Differences*. New York: WH Freeman.

Soucie, D. G. (1982) 'Management Theory and Practice', in Zeigler,

E. F. *Physical Education and Sport: an Introduction.* Philadelphia: Lea and Febiger.

Southworth, G. (1998) *Leading Improving Primary Schools – The Work of Headteachers and Deputy Heads.* London: Falmer.

Spackman, L. (1998). 'Assessment and Recording in Physical Education', *British Journal of Physical Education,* **29** (4), 6–9.

Span, P. (1995) 'Self-regulated Learning by Highly Able Children' in Freeman, J., Span, P. and Wagner, H. (eds) *Actualizing Talent: a Lifelong Challenge.* London: Cassell.

Speednet (1999) 'Primary School PE Survey' in *British Journal of Physical Education,* **30** (3), 19–20.

Sports Council (1993) *Young People and Sport.* London: Sports Council.

Stidder, G. (2000) 'GCSE Physical Education for All: A Step in the Right Direction?' *Bulletin of Physical Education,* **36** (2), 159–78.

Stidder, G. (2001) 'Curriculum Innovation at Key Stage 4: A Review of GCSE PE Results in One English Secondary School', *Bulletin of Physical Education,* **37** (1), 25–46.

Sugden, D. (1991) 'PE: Movement in the Right Direction', *British Journal of Special Education,* **4**, 134–6.

Sugden, D. and Wright, H. (1996) 'Curricular Entitlement and Implementation for All Children' in Armstrong, N. (ed.) *New Directions in Physical Education: Change and Innovation.* London: Cassell.

Talbot, M. (1996) 'Gender and National Curriculum Physical Education', *British Journal of Physical Education,* **27** (1), 5–7.

Talbot, M. (2001) 'The Case for Physical Education', in Doll-Tepper, G. and Scoretz, D. (eds), *World Summit on Physical Education.* Berlin: ICSSPE.

Tannenbaum, A. J. (1983) *Gifted Children: Psychological and Educational Perspectives.* New York: Macmillan.

Tannenbaum, A. J. (1993) 'History of Giftedness and Gifted Education in World Perspective' in Heller, K. A., Monks, F. and Passow, A. H. (eds) *International Handbook of Research and Development of Giftedness and Talent.* Oxford: Pergamon.

Tannenbaum, R. and Schmidt, W. (1958) 'How to Choose a Leadership Pattern', *Harvard Business Review,* **36** (2), 95–101.

Tattum, D. (1982) *Disruptive Pupils in School and Units.* London: Wiley.

Teacher Training Agency (TTA) (1998) *National Standards for Subject Leaders.* London: TTA.

Tempest, N. R. (1974) *Teaching Clever Children 7–11*. London: Routledge and Kegan Paul.

The Guardian, 15/07/2000, 'Brown's Boost for School Sports', p. 7.

Thompson, L. (1998) 'Teaching Strategies to Enhance Motivation to Learn in Elementary Physical Education', *CAHPERD*, **64** (1), 4–10.

Torkildsen, G. (1996) *Leisure and Recreation Management*. London: E. and F. N. Spon.

Torrance, E. P. (1987), 'Teaching for Creativity' in Isaksen, S. G. (ed.) *Frontiers of Creativity Research*. New York: Bearly.

Treffinger, D. J. and Feldhusen, J. F. (1996) 'Talent Recognition and Development: Successor to Gifted Education' *Journal for the Education of the Gifted*, **19**, 181–93.

UNESCO (1994) *The Salamanca Statement and Framework for Action*. Paris: UNESCO.

Usher, P. (1997) 'Empowerment as a Powerful Coaching Tool', *Coaches' Report*, **4** (2), 10–11.

Van Tassel-Baska, J. (1994) *Comprehensive Curriculum for Gifted Learners*. Massachusetts: Allyn and Bacon.

Vanden Auweele, Y., Bakker, F., Biddle, S., Durand, M. and Seiler, R. (eds) (1999) *Psychology for Physical Educators*. Champaign, Ill.: Human Kinetics.

Vickerman, P. (1997) 'Knowing Your Pupils and Planning for Different Needs' in Capel, S. (ed.), *Learning to Teach Physical Education in the Secondary School*, London: Routledge.

Warburton, P. (1999) 'Our Sporting Nation – Have We Got the Agenda Right for Our Young People?', *British Journal of Physical Education*, **30** (1), 18–24.

Webb, J. T. (1993) 'Nurturing Social-emotional Development of Gifted Children' in Heller, K. A., Monks, F. J. and Passow, A. H. *International Handbook of Research and Development of Giftedness and Talent*. Oxford: Pergamon Press.

Weinberg, R. S. and Gould, D. (1995) *Foundations of Sport and Exercise Psychology*. Champaign, Ill.: Human Kinetics.

Weiss, M. and Duncan, S. (1992) 'The Relationship Between Physical Competence and Peer Acceptance in the Context of Children's Sports Participation', *Journal of Sport and Exercise Psychology*, **14** (2), 177–92.

Welch, A. (1978) *Accidents Happen*. London: John Murray.

Wetton, P. (1988) *Physical Education in the Nursery and Infant School*. London: Routledge.

WHO (1980) *International Classification of Impairments, Disabilities and Handicaps*. Geneva: World Health Organization.

Williams, A. (1989) *Issues in Physical Education for the Primary Years*. London: Falmer.

Williams, A. (1993) 'Aspects of Teaching and Learning Gymnastics', *British Journal of Physical Education*, **24** (1), 29–32.

Williams, A. (1996) *Teaching Physical Education – a Guide for Mentors and Students*. London: David Fulton.

Williams, A. M. and Reilly, T. (2000) 'Talent Identification and Development in Soccer', *Journal of Sports Sciences*, **18**, 657–67.

Winser, N. (1988) 'Aims, Objectives and Critical Path Planning' in Winser, N. and Winser, S. (eds) *Expedition Planners' Handbook and Directory 1988–89*. London: Expedition Advisory Centre.

Wragg, E. C. (ed.) (1984) *Classroom Teaching Skills*. London: Croom Helm.

Wragg, E. C. and Wood, E. K. (1984a) 'Teachers' First Encounters with their Classes' in Wragg, E. C. (ed.), *Classroom Teaching Skills*. London: Croom Helm.

Wragg, E. C. and Wood, E. K. (1984b) 'Pupil Appraisals of Teaching', in Wragg, E. C. (ed.), *Classroom Teaching Skills*. London: Croom Helm.

Wragg, E. C. (1993) *Primary Teaching Skills*. London: Routledge.

Wuest, D. A. and Bucher, C. A. (1995) *Foundations of Physical Education and Sport*. St Louis: Mosby-Year Book.

Young, P. and Tyre, E. (1992) *Gifted or Able?* Buckingham: Open University Press.

Index

Lightning Source UK Ltd.
Milton Keynes UK
UKOW040317030112

184621UK00004B/1/P